Teaching and Learning Grammar:

The Prototype- Construction Approach

Teaching and Learning Grammar:

The Prototype-
Construction
Approach

Arthur Whimbey
Myra Linden

BGF Performance Systems, LLC
Chicago, IL

2001

BGF Performance Systems, LLC
P.O. Box 256643
Chicago, IL 60625-6643
866-602-1477
www.bgfperformance.com

ISBN: 0-9709075-2-4

Cover design by Rojo Designs

Printed in the United States of America

DEDICATION

To Drs. Jerome Snyder and Mark Beauchamp of Lovelace Health Systems and Dr. Charles Stutzman of St. Joseph Cancer Center for helping Art fight cancer and thus making this book possible.

CONTENTS

ABOUT THE AUTHORS

Arthur Whimbey has authored such cutting edge books as *Intelligence Can Be Taught*, *Mastering Reading Through Reasoning*, and *Analyze Organize Write*. He is also the innovator of such instructional approaches as Thinking Aloud Problem Solving (TAPS), which has a very successful track record with Project SOAR of Xavier University, LA.

Myra Linden, a member of the National Council of Teachers of English, has taught English for over 35 years at the high school and college levels. She is the author of innovative books such as *Why Johnny Can't Write* and *Keys to Quick Writing Skills*, which explore the topic of what works and what doesn't work in modern writing instruction. She has spent much time researching successful techniques for improving writing and reading skills through immersing students in language usage.

CHAPTER

1

A TIME FOR CHANGE

This book describes a new approach to teaching grammar, the Prototype-Construction (P-C) Approach. The P-C Approach arose from a need for a better method to teach grammar because research studies, as well as personal experiences of students and teachers, all point to the conclusion that the current method is not very effective. For example, a report commissioned by the National Council of Teachers of English asserts:

> None of the studies reviewed for the present report provides any support for teaching grammar as a means of improving composition skills. If schools insist upon teaching the identification of parts of speech, the parsing or diagramming of sentences, or other concepts of traditional school grammar (as many still do), they cannot defend it as a means of improving the quality of writing.

The studies reviewed for the report used what is called the "traditional" approach to teaching grammar. The Prototype-Construction Approach differs from the traditional approach in both what is taught and how it is taught. The first part of its name (Prototype) reflects what is taught. The second part (Construction) focuses on how it is taught. We begin in the next chapter by discussing one of the major problems in traditional grammar: defining grammatical concepts. Then we explain how the P-C Approach deals with this problem.

Samples of the explanations and exercises presented to students in a P-C workbook are reprinted throughout this book. We suggest that you read the explanations and do all the exercises to obtain a firsthand view of how the various grammatical concepts are introduced to students, and how the exercises reinforce students' functional understanding of the concepts.

CHAPTER

2

THE PROBLEM: WHERE TO BEGIN TEACHING THE COMPLEXITIES OF GRAMMAR

I n *Grammar and Good Taste*, Dennis Baron, professor of English and linguistics at the University of Illinois, wrote of the difficulty he encountered trying to learn grammar:

> I clearly remember cowering at my desk in a ninth-grade English class while a certain Mrs. B— rained mysterious objects she called nouns and verbs at us like bombs. I finally mastered the parts of speech in graduate school, or so I thought until I found myself on the other side of the desk, standing before a New York City high school English class, Warriner's grammar book in hand, with instructions from my department head to teach a grammar lesson. The instantaneous Pavlovian glaze in my

students' eyes took me back again a dozen years.

The Warriner's grammar book mentioned by Baron is a widely used classic in the field. The reason that Baron experienced difficulty with the "mysterious objects she called…verbs" can be understood by examining the definition of a verb presented in this and most other popular grammar textbooks. The definition in such texts generally takes this form.

A verb is a word that expresses an action or a state of being.

One of the authors (Whimbey) remembers how this definition led to a bad grammar day during his own high school years. He recalls:

> **When I was in the 9th grade at Brooklyn Technical High School, my English teacher stood at the board and said, 'Your textbook defines a verb as a word that describes an action or state of being.' On the board she wrote:**
>
> **A verb describes an action or state of being.**
>
> **Next she wrote this sentence on the board:**
>
> **Eating custard pie, Peter is a picture of happiness.**
>
> **Then she called on me to identify the verb in the sentence.**
>
> **It seemed clear to me that *eating* expresses an action, so I answered, 'Eating.'**
>
> **To my surprise the teacher said, 'No, eating is not the verb.'**
>
> **I protested, 'But the book says a verb is an action word. Eating is an action.'**
>
> **The teacher responded with what was to her an apparently clear explanation: 'Yes, but eating is a participle, not the verb in this sentence.'**
>
> **I had no idea what a participle was, but I began looking for another action word in the sentence—without success.**
>
> **Sensing my frustration, the teacher offered a hint: 'Remember that a verb can describe a state of being.'**
>
> **State of being, I thought. What is a state of being?**
>
> **Scanning the sentence to find a word expressing a state of being, I considered *happiness*. *Happiness* seemed to express a state of being. I figured that if I knew what a verb was, I would be in a state of happiness. Unsure but hopeful, I asked, 'Is *happiness***

the verb?'

'No,' came the judgment.

After another minute or so, the teacher answered her own question:

'The verb in this sentence is *is*.'

But it didn't matter. Grammar made no sense to me, and I dismissed it as something I would never understand.

We will see in Chapter 4 why the teacher's hint was not very helpful.

Whimbey's guess that the noun *happiness* expresses a state was not totally wrong since some nouns, including *happiness*, do name states. In fact, the noun *ecstasy* is identified as a state in the next sentence.

> After the wedding announcement, the entire family remained in a *state of ecstasy* for weeks.

Furthermore, in the last sentence a beginning student could easily choose *announcement* as the word expressing an action and therefore conclude that it is the verb.

Here are four more sentences with underlined nouns expressing actions; a beginning student might pick them as the "action" words and thus the verbs. In the first sentence, *rapid* accentuates that *movement* is an action word, since actions may be rapid or slow.

> Rapid <u>movement</u> of an army requires careful <u>planning</u>.
> Her <u>screams</u> for help remained unanswered.
> His <u>leap</u> amazed the coach.
> The Norman <u>invasion</u> and <u>defeat</u> of England occurred in 1066.

In most school grammar textbooks, after students are presented with the above definition, they are told that verbs may be single words or phrases such as *should eat, was eaten, will have eaten,* and *has been eating.* Students are shown several sentences with the verbs and verb phrases underlined. Then they are given another group of sentences and told to underline the verb or verb phrase in each. Here are some typical sentences.

1. The cold, juicy peach tasted wonderful after our long hike in the summer heat.

2. The star of that movie owns his own plane and also a house in Malibu with a swimming pool shaped like a plane.

3. Before entering the Jacuzzi, you must take a shower.

4. The lion cub was rejected by its mother.

5. Are Kevin and Jerome recording their new CD today?

6. For baking potatoes, set the oven at 350 degrees.

7. Karen wants to go ice skating this weekend.

8. Mr. Robinson had been the assistant coach for ten years before being promoted to head coach.

Students generally find these exercises quite confusing, in some cases more so when they are shown the correct answers. For example, when they see that *must take* is the verb phrase in Sentence 3, they may have no idea how *must* fits into this mysterious scheme. Also, in Sentence 5, if they had chosen *recording* as the verb, they are told that they found only part of the verb, that the entire verb is *are recording*—because a verb is often split in a question. And in Sentence 7, they may be surprised to find that neither the action word *go* nor *skating* is the verb, but that for some reason *wants* has been designated as the answer by those in control of grades.

Identifying the verb in these sentences requires understanding various types of verb phrases and also the knowledge needed to distinguish between verbs and advanced grammatical structures that are related to verbs but play other roles in sentences. Few students ever come to understand these advanced structures under the traditional approach because they never have an opportunity to master the basics (such as simple verbs) which is a prerequisite for understanding the advanced topics. But the P-C Approach uses a "divide and conquer" strategy. First simple concepts called prototypes are taught to a level of mastery. With this foundation, students are prepared to learn more advanced concepts.

Under the traditional approach, even when students do correctly identify the verb in a sentence, often they are not sure why it is the verb. It just looks somewhat like the examples they were shown. With this approach, most students never really learn what a verb is. Mark Lester (referring to the grammar traditionally taught in schools as Grammar 4) writes in *Grammar for the Classroom*:

> **For most students in most classrooms, the study of Grammar 4 has not been successful. The very fact that all standard English textbooks repeat the same grammar material at each grade level tacitly acknowledges that no one really expects students to understand Grammar 4. In a kind of inoculation theory of education, Grammar 4 is repeated each year in the hope that**

this time it will 'take.' Most students have an extremely negative attitude toward schoolroom traditional grammar, rooted, I believe, in their frustration in not being able to understand it or to use it with much success in dealing with their own writing problems.

The definition of a verb presented above, the one found in most school grammar texts, is an inadequate oversimplification. A true definition of a verb is given in *Merriam Webster's Collegiate Dictionary*:

> a word that characteristically is the grammatical center of a predicate and that expresses an act, occurrence, or mode of being, that in various languages is inflected for agreement with the subject, for tense, for voice, for mood, or for aspect, and that typically has rather full descriptive meaning and characterizing quality but is sometimes nearly devoid of these esp. when used as an auxiliary or linking verb

However, this definition is too complicated to offer to beginning students. It includes a number of advanced grammatical terms and concepts, such as "inflected," "predicate," and "voice." Consequently, the persistent problem haunting grammar instruction has been where to start.

Another aspect of the problem is that the grammatical classification of a word often depends on the role it plays in a sentence. For instance, *water* is a noun playing the role of a subject in this sentence.

Water is necessary for life.

But *water* is a verb in the next sentence.

The Williams *water* their lawn every Saturday.

Similarly, *lectures* is the subject (a noun) in the first of the following sentences but a verb in the second.

His *lectures* bore most of the students.
He *lectures* without any feeling or enthusiasm in his voice.

Consequently, defining a subject or a verb may require specifying its role in a sentence. But all three of these words (*subject, verb*, and *sentence*) represent complicated grammatical concepts. Greenbaum and Quirk note that:

> Grammar is a complex system, the parts of which cannot be properly explained in abstraction from the whole. In this sense,

all parts of a grammar are mutually defining, and there is no simple linear path we can take in explaining one part in terms of another.

Thus, the problem that has plagued grammar instruction is how to introduce students to the subject so that they understand the basics and then progress to more advanced concepts. How can terms like *subject*, *verb*, and *predicate* be defined for students? In an article entitled "Forward to the Basics: Getting Down to Grammar," Robert DeBeaugrande expresses the problem as follows:

> **As long as school grammar is couched in vague and technical terms, it is not 'basic' enough to help students with genuine literacy problems, and we will achieve very little by going 'back' to it. Such grammar is like a ladder with the lower rungs taken out: the real beginner can't get anywhere. Students who don't happen to figure out by themselves, through lengthy induction, what the basic terms mean, won't profit much from grammatical instruction. If school grammar succeeded in past times, the student population was much narrower and more uniform than what we have today; it was much easier to rely on hidden presuppositions about things we couldn't explain very well.**

The next chapter describes a method that has proven effective for providing students with the "lower rungs" of the ladder—the first steps in understanding grammar.

CHAPTER
3

PROTOTYPE DEFINITIONS AND
CONSTRUCTION EXERCISES

R esearch by the authors revealed that many people who have a good grasp of grammar think of a basic verb as an action word and think of other verbs as words playing a grammatically analogous role in a sentence. Furthermore, they think of a basic sentence as having three main parts, along with other secondary parts. The three main parts are a subject that performs an action, a verb that expresses an action, and an object that receives the action. These findings, combined with a new theory of grammar explained in Chapter 19, suggested that an action verb could be regarded as a primary or "prototype" verb, and that the three-element sentence could be regarded as a "prototype" sentence. Furthermore, it suggested that these prototypes could serve as the door through which students could enter the world of grammar without confusion or anxiety. Students are told:

> Most written material, such as books and magazines, consist of sentences. Here is a basic sentence.
>
> Chefs prepare meals.
>   ↑   ↑   ↑
> subject verb   object
>
> This sentence has three parts: a subject, a verb, and an object. In this sentence, the subject performs an action. The verb expresses the action. And the object receives the action.

Note that students are not given a general definition of a verb, neither an oversimplified one nor a complicated one. Instead, they are told that a verb expresses an action in one type of basic sentence.

Next, this sentence is used to show that the subject and the verb must agree in number. Students are told:

> The subject in a sentence may be singular or plural. A singular subject refers to just one thing, while a plural subject refers to more than one thing. Generally, a subject is made plural by adding an *s* at the end.
>
> | | Subject |
> | -------- | ------- |
> | <u>Singular</u> | <u>Plural</u> |
> | chef | chef*s* |
>
> Verbs may also be singular or plural. But verbs are opposite to subjects in how they are made singular or plural. Adding an *s* to the end of a verb makes it singular.
>
> | | Verb |
> | -------- | ---- |
> | <u>Singular</u> | <u>Plural</u> |
> | prepare*s* | prepare |
>
> The verb in a sentence must agree with the subject in number. If the subject is singular, the verb must also be singular, as in the next sentence.
>
> Singular Subject and Verb: A chef prepare*s* meals.
>
> In the above sentence, the subject (*chef*) is singular so it does not end in *s*. The verb (*prepares*) is also singular, so it does end in *s*.
>
> If the subject is plural, the verb must also be plural. In the next sentence, the subject is plural, so it ends in *s*. The verb is also plural, so it does not

end in *s*.

Plural Subject and Verb: Chef*s* prepare meals.

You might think of this pattern as the S/No-S pattern. If you add an *s* to the subject, you do not add an *s* to the verb. But if you do not add an *s* to the subject, then you do add an *s* to the verb. Use this pattern in the following exercises.

Exercises

1. The following sentence has a singular subject and verb.
    Rewrite it with a plural subject and verb.

    Singular: A plane burns fuel.

    Plural: _____

2. The following sentence has a plural subject and verb. Rewrite it with a singular subject and verb.

    Plural: Potholes damage tires.

    Singular: _____

Exceptions to this pattern (such as the plural of *man* being *men*) are also explained to students.

Merriam Webster's definition reprinted in Chapter 2 says a verb "is inflected for agreement with the subject." *Inflect* means "change form." In the above exercises, students inflect verbs to agree with the subject, ensuring that they understand this characteristic of verbs. While only one exercise for a singular verb and one for a plural verb are shown above, the grammar workbook we developed presents five exercises of each type, so that students whose language habits differ from Standard Written English (SWE) can practice this inflection pattern. In addition, all the sentences that students construct and write in the remainder of the workbook use the subject-verb agreement pattern of SWE, so that even for lessons on other grammatical topics, such as adding adjectives or participial phrases to sentences, students are actively immersed in correct verb usage. Based on research findings, neuroscientists have coined an adage: Neurons which fire together, wire together. When students repeatedly write sentences with correct subject-verb combinations, these combinations become neurologically ingrained and habitual.

The next lesson deals with another part of Merriam Webster's definition, namely, inflection for tense. Students are told:

Notice how the verb is changed in the following sentences to state that the action took place in the past

Present: Swimmers lift weights.

Past: Swimmers lifted weights.

To show that an action took place in the past, generally *ed* is added to the end of the verb (or just *d* if the verb ends in *e*).

Students do several exercises using this principle.

Next the Prototype-Construction Approach begins introducing students to verbs that differ from prototype verbs. First students are shown that irregular verbs may change form in different ways to indicate past action. They complete several exercises changing verbs like *eat* to *ate* and *drive* to *drove*. Then students work with intransitive verbs, noting that they are not followed by objects but, nevertheless, have the same inflection patterns as transitive verbs. Finally, students are introduced to verbs that do not express action:

A verb in a sentence does not always express an action. Consider this sentence.

My brother owns a plane.

Owns is not really an action. However, *owns* is the verb in this sentence because it plays a grammatical role similar to the verbs you worked with in the previous exercises. It follows the subject, and it changes in the same way that action verbs change to show that the subject is singular or plural.

Singular: My brother owns a plane.

Plural: My brothers own a plane.

This verb also changes in the same way as action verbs to show that the sentence refers to the past.

Past: My brother owned a speedboat.

Verbs such as *own* are called "statives" because they generally represent a static situation rather than an action. Other statives are illustrated in the following exercises.

Chapter 2 notes that most school grammar texts show students various types of verb phrases (*will be eating, has been eaten*) right after presenting the oversimplified definition of a verb. The P-C Approach does not introduce verb phrases until students have practiced inflecting action verbs, irregular verbs, intransitive verbs, and statives. Only then does it introduce a verb phrase, one of the simplest—using *will* to write about the future. Here is the explanation given to students.

> English verbs have a distinct form to show past tense. Generally the past tense is written by adding *ed* to the base form of the verb. But English verbs do not have a distinct form to show future tense. Instead, the helping verb *will* is placed before the base form of the verb to indicate future tense. Compare these sentences.
>
> > Doris attends college.
> >
> > Doris *will attend* college.
>
> The first sentence makes a statement about the present. The second sentence makes a statement about the future.
>
> *Will* is called a helping verb. A helping verb is a word used along with a main verb to extend its meaning.
>
> The pair of words *will attend* is a verb phrase. A "phrase" is two or more words used together to play some role in a sentence.
>
> When the helping verb *will* precedes a main verb, the base form of the main verb is always used. This is true whether the subject of a sentence is singular or plural.
>
> > Singular Subject: An architect will design our new home.
> >
> > Plural Subject: Two architects will design our new home.

Exercise

> Rewrite this sentence so that it makes a statement about the future.
>
> Past: Bessie bought Larry's motorcycle.
>
> Future: _____

The series of instructions and exercises presented above illustrates the P-C Approach. The P-C Approach recognizes that grammatical concepts are too complex to fit oversimplified definitions. It also recognizes that the full range of verbs and other grammatical concepts is too complicated to throw at students all at once. It views each grammatical concept as including relatively simple "prototype" cases that can readily be defined and also more complicated, harder-to-define cases. It begins by introducing students to the prototype cases. Next it provides exercises that show students the grammatical characteristics of the prototypes. Then it introduces non-prototype cases which do not fit the simple definitions describing the prototypes, but it provides additional exercises to show that these cases have some similar grammatical characteristics and therefore belong in the same grammatical category.

The P-C Approach differs from the traditional approach not only in how it defines concepts but also in what it asks students to do. In the traditional approach, students are generally asked to identify the words in a sentence according to their grammatical classification—verb or noun, subject or predicate. But a great deal of research in which students were asked to manipulate and write sentences showed that these activities are more effective for improving writing skills. This research is summarized in *Why Johnny Can't Write: How to Improve Writing Skills* by Linden and Whimbey. Therefore, the P-C Approach asks students to manipulate grammatical concepts, and then construct and write sentences. The exercises shown above involve very simple sentence manipulations. But the following chapters will illustrate exercises that teach an array of grammatical concepts and involve more complex sentences and manipulations. Teachers have reported good results using workbooks that were developed by the present authors and that include various types of exercises in which students have to manipulate and write sentences. For example, Nathan Crow, principal of the Littleton Preparatory Charter School, wrote:

> Using *Analyze, Organize, Write* and similar exercises with a wide range of students, I obtained gains of between 3.0 grade levels and 6.2 grade levels per year of instruction, as assessed by the Woodcock/Johnson Revised 'writing sample' test.

CHAPTER
4

A UNIQUE FAMILY OF VERBS: IS, WAS, ARE, WERE, AM, BE, BEEN, BEING

A *Common Yet Complicated Verb*

Traditional grammar textbooks discuss the family of verbs that includes *is* and *was* together with action verbs like *cook* and *bake*. This practice has added to the confusion that students experience in trying to learn grammar. The P-C Approach deals with this family of verbs separately because it is the most complicated group of verbs in the English language and therefore the most troublesome for many students. This family of verbs differs from all other verbs in several ways:

1. It is the only family with three present tense forms: AM, IS, ARE.

2. It is the only family with two past tense forms: WAS, WERE.

3. It is the only family whose base form is not one of its present tense forms. Its base form is BE.

4. It expresses a unique meaning that is misrepresented in most traditional grammar textbooks.

Let us begin with the common verb *is*. The verb *is* is similar to other verbs in changing form to show whether the subject is singular or plural. But it differs from other verbs because its singular and plural forms are completely different words. The plural form of *is* is *are*.

Singular	Plural
A boy *is* outside.	Two boys *are* outside.

The verb *is* is also similar to other verbs in changing form to show that a sentence refers to the past. But it differs from other verbs because *ed* is not added to the base verb, nor is the word itself changed slightly, as with most irregular verbs. Instead, a completely different word is used. The past form of the singular verb *is* is *was*.

Singular
Present: A boy *is* outside.
Past: A boy *was* outside.

With a plural subject, yet another word is used. The past form of *are* is *were*.

Plural
Present: Two boys are outside.
Past: Two boys *were* outside.

The following tables contrast the verbs *is* and *bake*.

	Is		Bake	
	Singular	Plural	Singular	Plural
Present:	is	are	bakes	bake
Past:	was	were	baked	baked

There is even another present tense form of *is* that will be discussed shortly.

In our P-C workbook, after the above information is explained to students, they are asked to complete exercises which help ensure that they understand, remember, and can use the verb forms correctly in constructing sentences.

Future Tense and the Base Form Be

Some grammar textbooks tell students that *is* and *was* are forms of the verb *be* without explaining why this terminology is used. What do *is* and *was* have to do with *be*? To see the connection between *is* and *be*, let us consider writing sentences about the future. Recall from Chapter 3 that sentences about the future use the helping verb *will* and the base form of the main verb:

> Present: Martha *makes* tamales.
> Future: Martha *will make* tamales.

Here is a sentence that contains *is* and concerns the present.

> Present: George *is* happy.

Using our knowledge of English, let us transform this sentence to make a statement about the future and see what form the verb takes.

> Future: George *will be* happy.

Since the helping verb *will* is followed by *be*, this suggests that *be* is the base form for this family of verbs. Let us now try a case using the plural verb *are*.

> Present: The twins *are* boy scouts.

Transforming this into a statement about the future produces the following sentence.

> Future: The twins *will be* boy scouts.

Again we see that *be* is apparently the base form for *is* and *are*. In later chapters on modals and infinitives, we will find additional evidence for concluding that the base form for this family of verbs is *be*.

A family of verbs is often referred to by its base form. The verbs *eat, eats, ate, eating*, and *eaten* are said to be forms of the verb *eat*. Throughout the rest of this book, we will refer to the entire family that includes *is, are, was, were, am, be, been*, and *being* as *be* verbs. Thus, we will make statements such as the following: The singular forms of *be* are *is, was*, and *am*.

The Progressive Tenses

We have not yet discussed three forms of be: *am*, *been*, and *being*. *Am* and *been* will be discussed later. The form *being* is used in progressive tenses. Let us now illustrate how the progressive tenses are introduced to students in our P-C workbook. Students are told:

> So far in this chapter, forms of the verb *be* have been used as main verbs in sentences. However, the forms of *be* play another important role in English. They are used as helping verbs. This means that they are used in combination with other verbs (main verbs) to give the other verbs somewhat different meanings. One use of *be* as a helping verb is in forming the "progressive tenses." To begin our discussion of the progressive tenses, compare these sentences.
>
> > Jack chews gum.
> > Jack is chewing gum.
>
> The verb *chews* in the first sentence is called a *present tense verb*. But this label is only an approximation. Such a sentence is often used for a statement that is true regularly or continuously rather than at just this moment. The second sentence is the type of sentence generally used to say that something is happening now. Instead of just the verb *chews*, the sentence has the verb phrase *is chewing*. The verb phrase *is chewing* consists of the helping verb *is* and the base form of the main verb *chew* with *ing* added to the end. A verb phrase like *is chewing* is said to be in the *progressive tense*. The term "progressive" is used because the sentence describes an action that is "in progress." It is an action occurring right now.

Students are asked to try the following sample exercise.

Sample Exercise

Rewrite the following sentence with the verb in the present progressive tense.

> Present: The Mississippi River *overflows* its banks in New Orleans.
>
> Progressive: _____

Answer Explanation

To write the verb in the present progressive tense, insert the helping verb *is* and add *ing* to the base form of the main verb. The main verb is *overflows*. Its base form is *overflow*. Therefore, the *ing* form is *overflowing*.

> Progressive: The Mississippi River *is overflowing* its banks in New Orleans.

Students are asked to complete several exercises in which they transform sentences with present tense verbs into sentences with present progressive verbs. Then they are shown that *are* is used as the helping verb if the subject is plural, and that *was* or *were* is used to create sentences with past progressive verbs.

Now consider this sentence.

Jimmy is a naughty boy.

To transform this into a sentence with a present progressive verb, we need to insert *is,* and we also need to add *ing* to the base form of the main verb. The main verb is *is.* The base form of *is* is *be.* Therefore, the *ing* form is *being.* Here is the sentence with a present progressive verb.

Jimmy *is being* a naughty boy.

All verbs have an *ing* form. Technically, the *ing* form is called the *present participle.* The *ing* form of *be* is *being.* We will come back to present participles in a later chapter.

The Form Am

In order to explain *am* to students, we first explain that in grammar, the writer is considered the "first person," the reader is the "second person," and all other people or things are the "third person." Furthermore, when the subject of a sentence is the first person, the appropriate present tense form of *be* is *am.* This is shown in the first of the following sentences.

First Person: I *am* a good teacher.
Second Person: You are a good teacher.
Third Person: Judy is a good teacher.

Students are shown several more examples, and then the past tense forms of *be* for the first, second, and third person are discussed. Next, students are asked to try the following sample exercise.

Sample Exercise

Rewrite the following sentence with a first person subject (*I*) and the appropriate present tense form of *be.*

Third Person: Tom is an optimist.

First Person: _____

Answer Explanation

The present tense form of *be* for a first person subject is *am*.

First Person: I *am* an optimist.

Finally, students are asked to complete a number of similar exercises.

The only form of *be* that we have not discussed is *been*. We do not introduce students to *been* until we can do so meaningfully in a later chapter on the perfect tenses, which use verb phrases such as *has been* and *had been*.

The Meaning of Be

Exactly what does *be* mean? Recall from chapter 2 that a high school English teacher asked Whimbey to find the verb in this sentence.

Eating custard pie, Peter is a picture of happiness.

When Whimbey had difficulty finding the verb, she gave him the following hint: "Remember that a verb can describe a state of being." She thought this hint would help him identify *is* as the verb.

Does *is* describe or express a state of being? Consider this simpler sentence.

Paul *is* confused.

This sentence says that Paul is in a state of confusion. However, *is* does not express the state. *Confused* expresses the state.

Here are two similar examples.

Maria *is* angry.

Gilbert *is* envious.

Angry expresses Maria's state, and *envious* expresses Gilbert's. What then does *is* express? The verb *is* indicates that what follows describes Maria and Gilbert. More broadly, *be* does not express a state but a statement, namely: What follows characterizes the subject. The verb *be* is simply a connector. It connects the subject with a word or phrase that expresses some information about the subject. Here are two other sentences with *be*.

Mr. Williams *is* our football coach.

Bob *is* in the garage.

In both cases the phrase to the right of *is* presents information about the subject. *Be* is just a connector. Of course, like all verbs, *be* does carry tense, so that distinctions can be made between information about the subject currently, and information concerning the past or future:

Mr. Williams *is* our football coach.

Mr. Williams *was* our football coach.

Mr. Williams *will be* our football coach.

Occasionally *be* is used with another meaning. Many words have more than one meaning. A *suit* is an item of clothing consisting of a jacket and a pair of pants. But a *suit* is also a legal action—a *law suit*. The verb *be* means "exists" in this sentence: There *is* no escape. In fact, *exists* can replace *be* in the sentence: There *exists* no escape. Here is one of Shakespeare's most famous lines:

To be, or not to be: that is the question.

In this context, *be* again means "live" or "exist." But even for this usage, it might not be appropriate to say that *be* expresses a state, since the term *state* is so broad. Instead, in this usage, *be* means "exist" or "live."

Furthermore, the use of *be* to mean "exist" is quite rare compared to its use as a connector between the subject and a word or phrase characterizing the subject. In this more common use, *be* definitely does not express a state. Thus, when traditional grammar textbooks suggest that *be* expresses a state, they just add to the confusion that many students experience in trying to learn grammar.

CHAPTER
5

NOUNS

Nouns are one of the easiest grammatical concepts to understand and teach. Nevertheless, defining a noun and some related concepts, such as a proper noun and a possessive form of a noun, involve complications that can confuse students if the complications are not explained clearly and the concepts are not defined accurately.

Traditional grammar texts define a noun as a word that names a person, place, or thing. There are two problems with this definition. First, we generally regard a "thing" as an object, such as a toy or a car. However, nouns can name mental states (*sadness*), physical states (*poverty*), actions (*defeat*), qualities (*softness*), and concepts (*democracy*). Including words such as *sadness, softness,* and *democracy* under the term *thing* is stretching the definition of *thing* somewhat. To be more descriptive, a noun could be defined as a word that names a person, place, concrete thing, state, action, quality, or concept.

The second weakness of the traditional definition is that some words are nouns only when they are used as nouns in sentences. For instance, *defeat* is a noun (subject) in the first sentence but a verb in the second.

> The *defeat* of Rome marked the end of cultural progress in Western Europe for several centuries.

> The Jets *defeat* the Alligators whenever they play in Reno.

Therefore, we must add a phrase such as the following to the definition:

> and that can serve as a subject in a sentence.

This addition distinguishes between *defeat* used as a noun and *defeat* used as a verb. Thus, the definition of a noun takes this form:

> A noun is a word that names a person, place, concrete thing, state, action, quality, or concept and that can serve as a subject in a sentence.

Nouns are also used as objects (and other elements) in sentences. But since words that can be subjects can also be objects, objects need not be mentioned in the above theoretical definition. However, objects are mentioned in explaining nouns to students.

Nouns that name persons, places, and concrete things may be considered prototype nouns. They include simple, common examples of the concept *noun*. We present a table of such nouns in introducing students to nouns. We then explain that some nouns name more abstract ideas, and we provide exercises to familiarize students with more abstract nouns. Students are told:

> In the chapter on action verbs, you wrote sentences containing subjects and objects. The kinds of words that can be used as subjects and objects are called nouns. Some nouns represent people, places, and everyday things. Here are some nouns.

> Nouns

> | People | Places | Things |
> |--------|--------|--------|
> | girl | Texas | ball |
> | man | city | fish |
> | George | Disneyland | Buick |
> | doctor | cellar | hamburger |

Nouns also name ideas and feelings, such as *freedom* and *happiness*. When you write sentences, the subjects and objects may be concrete nouns representing people and things, as illustrated in Sentence 1. Or they may be abstract nouns representing feelings and concepts, as in Sentence 2.

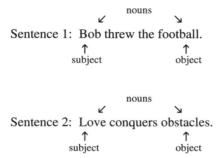

The table above presents a sample of concrete nouns. The next exercise illustrates abstract nouns naming a mental state, a physical state, an action, a characteristic, and a concept.

Exercise

Here are five nouns.

    honesty   prejudice   gravity   discovery   captivity

Below are five sentences with the subject positions left blank. Rewrite the sentences using each of the above nouns just once to fill the subject positions.

1. The _____ of penicillin has saved countless lives.

2. _____ is a human characteristic that is praised by society.

3. _____ is a physical state involving involuntary confinement.

4. _____ is a mental state characterized by a negative opinion towards something, often some group, without any reasonable grounds for the opinion or a willingness to change the opinion on the basis of facts.

5. _____ is a concept formulated by Newton to explain why unsupported objects fall to the earth instead of the sky.

Possessive Forms of Nouns

One characteristic that distinguishes nouns from verbs is that nouns can have a possessive form. The possessive form is generally written by adding an apostrophe and an *s* at the end. For example, the possessive form of the noun *Fred* is *Fred's*. The possessive form often indicates ownership, as expressed by this sentence.

Fred's car is the car owned by Fred.

↖

Possessive form of noun

However, the possessive form can indicate various other relationships. Perhaps the most unusual one is illustrated by *dog's owner*, as in this sentence:

The *dog's owner* is in that store.

What makes this usage of the possessive odd is that it reverses the meaning of the possessive. The dog does not own its owner. Quite the opposite. But this is just one of the vagaries of the language which students should learn in coming to understand that each grammatical concept has prototype cases (such as true ownership for possessive nouns) and also non-prototype cases with different meanings or forms.

We show students some of the other relationships that the possessive form can express, and then we ask students to complete exercises illustrating them. Here is what we present to students for five of the relationships. The answer for the first exercise is shown.

Relationships Expressed by Possessive Forms of Nouns

Relationship 1. The possessive noun may represent the author, creator, or originator of something.

> Example: Hemingway's prose is a paragon of efficient communication.

Exercise: Rewrite this sentence with the underlined phrase transformed into a phrase containing a possessive noun.

> The plays of Shakespeare have been popular for centuries.

> Answer: *Shakespeare's plays* have been popular for centuries.

Relationship 2. The possessive noun may represent an organization or entity employing someone.

> Example: *Germany's ambassador* to the United States will arrive tomorrow.

Exercise: Rewrite this sentence with the underlined phrase transformed into a phrase containing a possessive noun.

> The governor of California may be forced to resign because of the scandal.

Relationship 3. The possessive noun may represent the performer of an action.

Example: Wilson's touchdown won the game for the Raiders

Exercise: Rewrite this sentence with the underlined phrase transformed into a phrase containing a possessive noun.

The barking of the dog disturbed the neighbors.

Relationship 4. The possessive noun may indicate that what follows is a characteristic of the thing named by the noun.

Example: *The car's acceleration* is impressive but unnecessary.

Exercise: Rewrite this sentence with the underlined phrase transformed into a phrase containing a possessive noun.

The size of the computer makes it impractical to take on business trips.

Relationship 5. The possessive noun can indicate a unit of time.

Example: *A day's work* will be needed to repair the damage.

Exercise: Rewrite this sentence with the underlined phrase transformed into a phrase containing a possessive noun.

It would take the wages of a year for me to pay for that car.

Proper Nouns

Students are often told that a "proper" noun refers to one particular thing, and that the first letter of a proper noun is therefore capitalized. Furthermore, they are told that a "common" noun refers to many things, and its first letter is not capitalized unless it is the first word in a sentence. This explains why the first letter of *Mexico* is capitalized, since there is only one country named Mexico. But why is the *m* in Moscow capitalized? The capital of Russia is the best known city with this name, but there are also Moscows in Idaho, Pennsylvania, Texas, Minnesota, and a handful of other states. For instance, some years ago the good people of Greenville, Texas, could not get a post office because they were too close to another city named Greenville that had a post office, so they gave their community a new name—the name of a city they knew was definitely not close, a city in far off Russia: Moscow. Yet these people capitalized the new name of their city, in spite of knowing that another city already bore the name Moscow. Were they wrong in doing so?

Let's look at a few more cases. The word *boy* is not capitalized. It is said to be a common noun rather than a proper noun because it refers to all boys, not just one boy. The name *Tom*, on the other hand, is capitalized. However, there are many *Toms* in the world, so *Tom* does not refer to one specific boy. But there are fewer *Toms* than *boys* so the proper noun *Tom* is more specific than the common noun *boy*, just as the proper noun *Moscow* is more specific than the common noun *city*. On this basis, we might conclude that a proper noun is capitalized because it is more specific than a common noun. But this is still not the whole story. *German* and *French* are considered proper nouns and capitalized because they name specific languages. Yet *biology* and *physics* are not capitalized even though they name specific sciences. If *German* is capitalized, shouldn't *biology* be also? Thus, we see there is a certain arbitrariness in the convention governing the capitalization of words. In fact, *biology* is capitalized when it is part of the name for a college course, such as *Biology 101*.

To give students a more accurate understanding of which words are considered proper nouns and are therefore capitalized, we explain the different types of words that are considered proper nouns. After each type of proper noun is explained, students are asked to do an exercise in which they capitalize the proper noun. Here are the explanations for three types of proper nouns and their accompanying exercises. The answer for the first exercise is shown.

1. The names of persons and pets are proper nouns.

Exercise. Rewrite this sentence with the first letters of the two proper nouns capitalized.

> This afternoon marty and princess (our new kitten) took a nap together.
>
> Answer: This afternoon Marty and Princess (our new kitten) took a nap together.

2. The title of a government official is capitalized only when it precedes the name of the person holding the office. The one exception is the word president, which is always capitalized when it refers to the President of the United States.

Exercise. Rewrite this sentence with one more word capitalized.

> I believe that governor Johnson is the best governor we have had in the last two decades.

3. The points of the compass (*north*, *southwest*) are capitalized when

they name a region but not when they indicate a direction. In Sentence 1 below, *Southwest* names a region, just as *Texas* names a region. But in 2, *southwest* indicates a direction.

1. I love the food of the *Southwest*.

2. We drove *southwest* for two hours.

Exercise. Rewrite this sentence with the two words naming an area of the country treated as a proper noun.

We drove west for nine hours until we reached the west coast.

There are a number of additional rules governing capitalization that can be taught to students. By helping students understand these rules and apply them in exercises, instead of just giving them the traditional definition that "a proper noun names one specific thing," we encourage students to think about grammar rather than try only to memorize the right answers (whether or not they make sense) or simply give up on grammar. We encourage students to view the English language as a system they can master and use to express their own ideas.

CHAPTER

6

ADJECTIVES

A djectives allow a writer to bring sentences to life with vivid details. Here is a bare-bones sentence.

For dessert I had a peach.

Adding four adjectives makes the dessert much more enjoyable.

For dessert I had a delicious, sweet, ripe, juicy peach.
                                ↖   ↑   ↑   ↗
                                     adjectives

Showing students how to enrich their sentences with adjectives is fairly easy. However, teaching adjectives with the traditional approach can confuse students. First let us look at some typical adjective lessons using the P-C Approach. Then we will examine the difficulties that the traditional approach encounters because of its assumptions and goals. The P-C workbook tells students

> Adjectives can be used to describe things by naming their characteristics. The word *large* is an adjective in this sentence.
>
> A *large* dog followed me home.
>
> ↗   ↖
>
> adjective   noun
>
> The noun *dog* names an animal. The adjective *large* provides more information about the dog. It describes the dog by naming one of its characteristics (*large*).
>
> The adjective *large* is said to "modify" the noun *dog*. In grammar, "modify" means "add information to." The word *modify* is used because an adjective may change or "modify" your picture of something. If you are told that your neighbor just bought a dog, you may picture an average-sized dog. If you are told it is a small dog, your picture of the dog changes in one way, whereas being told it is a large dog modifies your picture differently. The adjective "modifies" your picture of the dog.
>
> An adjective is often placed before the noun it modifies, just as *large* is placed before *dog* in the sentence above. However, sometimes a verb like *is* or *are* (a form of *be*) is used to connect a noun with an adjective, as in this sentence.
>
> The house is old.
>
> ↗   ↖
>
> noun   adjective
>
> The adjective *old* describes the house,
>
> In the following exercises, you will add adjectives to sentences in order to provide more information about nouns. Try this sample exercise.

Sample Exercise

> Rewrite the first sentence with the adjectives from the other two sentences inserted before the nouns they modify.
>
> A storm can destroy a boat.
> The storm is violent.
> The boat is light.

Answer Explanation

> Step 1. The adjective *violent* describes the storm. So it is inserted before the noun *storm*.
>
> A *violent* storm can destroy a boat.

Step 2.The adjective *light* describes the boat, so it is inserted before the noun *boat*.

A violent storm can destroy a *light* boat.

After students complete several similar exercises, they are shown how two adjectives can modify the same noun:

Two adjectives can be used to modify the same noun, as in this sentence.

A *warm, dry* climate reduces the pain of arthritis.

The adjectives *warm* and *dry* modify the noun *climate*. Note that a comma has been placed between the adjectives. In the following exercises, place a comma between the two adjectives that you use to modify a noun.

Exercises

1. Rewrite the first sentence with the adjectives from the other sentences inserted before the noun they modify.

    Our commitment is to provide customers with transportation.
    The transportation is safe.
    The transportation is reliable.

2. In this exercise you will add adjectives to several nouns. Rewrite the first sentence with the adjectives from the other sentences inserted before the nouns they modify.

    Paul felt that the canyon was the setting for his novel.
    The canyon was silent.
    The canyon was empty.
    The setting was perfect.
    The novel was new.

Next, the workbook discusses the types of information that adjectives can provide, and the bearing that this has on comma usage.

Adjectives can provide information on many characteristics of an object, such as its size, shape, color, origin, material, and the impression it makes on the writer. An adjective signifying a material, such as *woolen*, is generally placed closer to a noun it modifies than other adjectives, as illustrated by this sentence.

Paula decided to wear a *red woolen* sweater.

Note that there is no comma between *red* and *woolen*. Note also that you would not normally write these adjectives in the opposite order.

Unusual: Paula decided to wear a *woolen red* sweater.

A comma is not needed between a pair of adjectives that would not normally be written in the reverse order. You will not need a comma between the adjectives that you add in the next exercise.

Exercise

Rewrite the first sentence with the adjectives from the other sentences inserted before the noun they modify.

> My cousin loves food.
> The food is spicy.
> The food is Spanish.

Finally, some alternative positions for adjectives are shown to students:

In the following sentence, two adjectives (*soft, cuddly*) modify the noun *kitten*.

> The *soft, cuddly* kitten was fed milk from a bottle for two weeks.

Sometimes two adjectives can be placed after the noun they modify, as shown in the next sentence.

The kitten, *soft* and *cuddly*, was fed milk from a bottle for two weeks.

↖ ↗

commas

Note that the two adjectives are set off with commas and connected with *and*. In your own writing, occasionally placing adjectives after nouns will add variety to your sentence patterns. It will also allow you to emphasize the adjectives more strongly. Try this exercise.

Exercise

Rewrite this sentence with the adjectives modifying *children* moved after *children*. Set the adjectives off with commas and connect them with *and*.

> The inexperienced, undernourished children should not have been working in the factory where the accident occurred.

The next lesson shows another interesting position for adjectives:

One way to emphasize a word is to place it in a different position from where it is normally found in a sentence. In English, a single adjective normally appears right before the noun it modifies. For instance, the adjective *famished* is right before the noun *hikers* in the next sentence.

> The famished hikers ate all the sandwiches we had prepared.

The adjective *famished* could be moved to the front of the sentence to draw more attention to it.

Famished, the hikers ate all the sandwiches we had prepared.

↖

comma

Note that *famished* is set off with a comma.

Exercise

Rewrite this sentence with the adjective *frustrated* moved to the front and set off with a comma.

> The frustrated engineers decided to quit for the day and begin working on the problem again in the morning.

The above lessons illustrate that showing students how to use adjectives for enriching their sentences is relatively easy. Nevertheless, traditional grammar fails to teach adjectives effectively because of its underlying assumptions and goals. One assumption is that all words can be classified into the following eight parts of speech: noun, pronoun, adjective, verb, adverb, preposition, conjunction, and interjection. This assumption dates back to antiquity but is not supported by modern linguistic research.

The second assumption is that teaching students to classify every word of a sentence into these eight parts of speech will improve their writing skills. Therefore, the goal of traditional grammar is to teach students to parse or diagram sentences in a way that classifies every word into the eight parts of speech.

A problem that these assumptions produce for traditional grammar is illustrated by the following sentence.

> *The* boys bought the *first three* bikes I showed them.

In terms of the eight parts of speech, what should the word *the* be called? It is not a noun, pronoun, verb, adverb, preposition, conjunction, or interjection. Furthermore, it occurs before the noun *boys*, and adjectives occur before nouns, so traditional grammar classifies *the* as an adjective. However, *the* does not describe the boys; therefore, it is very different from other adjectives. In fact, it is so different that modern linguists give *the*, along with *a* and *an*, a separate category called *articles*. Furthermore, articles are part of another category that modern grammarians call *determiners*.

Two other words in the above sentence are *first* and *three*. Which of the eight parts of speech are these words? Traditional grammar also classifies them as adjectives. However, many modern linguists recognize that numbers are very different from typical adjectives and therefore classify numbers as a separate group.

Furthermore, there are other words, such as *this* and *that* in the next sentence, which some traditional grammar books say are playing the role of adjectives.

This cup is mine and *that* cup is yours.

The result is that traditional grammar books must give students an unnecessarily complicated definition of adjectives, and therefore students receive only a fuzzy picture of what adjectives are and do. Since traditional grammar includes articles and numbers (and sometimes other words) among adjectives, it cannot simply tell students that adjectives may describe objects by naming their characteristics. It cannot just say that adjectives answer the question *what kind*, which is what adjectives like *small*, *woolen*, and *Spanish* do. Instead, it must say that adjectives answer the questions *what kind, how many,* and *which one.*

What is ironic about the situation is that most students whose native language is English do not have much difficulty with articles, so there is no need to "teach" articles in an introductory grammar course. Those students who do omit or misuse articles generally improve through the immersion in standard written English that the P-C Approach provides by having students write complete sentences in each exercise. In any case, telling weak students that articles are adjectives does not help them.

Since the goal of the P-C Approach is not to teach students to classify every word in a sentence but to use various grammatical structures for expressing ideas, it is not required to deal with articles and numbers, but can focus on the effective use of descriptive adjectives.

In the October 1995 issue of *Composition Chronicle*, the editor, Bill McCleary, observed that a new and effective pedagogical grammar was needed, one that would suggest which grammatical concepts should be taught and how they should be taught to improve students' writing skills. The P-C Approach is one attempt to meet that need.

Casey,
Our # is
410 461-7058
Janna + Sue,
Sam

ER

/

ADVERBS

A dverbs play many roles in sentences, perhaps too many. Modern linguists contend that traditional grammarians put too many different types of words into the adverb category because they assume that English can be fully described with just eight parts of speech. The result of this questionable assumption is that traditional grammar textbooks present an oversimplified definition of adverbs coupled with inadequate instruction on the different types of adverbs. This situation has left students with a fuzzy understanding of what adverbs are and how they can be used effectively.

Most traditional grammar textbooks give students the following definition of an adverb.

> *An adverb is a word that modifies a verb, an adjective, or another adverb.*

Already we see that a complication has raised its troublesome head. The definition says that adverbs modify not only verbs but also adjectives and other adverbs. Herein lies the first difficulty that students experience with traditional grammar. Traditional textbooks generally do not devote enough attention to teaching the two types of adverbs separately: They do not first discuss adverbs that modify verbs, letting students add these to sentences, and then discuss adverbs that modify adjectives and other adverbs, providing practice with them.

But that is only the beginning of the problem. Traditional grammarians include in the adverb category a diverse group of words that, according to modern linguists, do not modify verbs, adjectives, or other adverbs. Some seem to modify clauses or sentences, and others may not modify anything but simply add more information to a sentence. Therefore, they do not fit the definition given to students. The result: Students experience the hopeless confusion that Dennis Baron describes in his recollection of learning and teaching grammar (quoted in Chapter 2).

Let us begin a survey of the various types of adverbs by reviewing how the P-C Approach introduces students to prototype adverbs. Students are told:

In the following sentence, *quickly* describes the action *ran*.

Paul ran *quickly* down the stairs.

Quickly adds information to the verb *ran*. Therefore, *quickly* is said to "modify" *ran*. Just as an adjective modifies a noun by adding information to it, *quickly* modifies *ran*. A word that modifies a verb is called an adverb. *Hesitantly* is an adverb in the next sentence.

Charlie *hesitantly* tasted the turtle soup
↑
adverb

Just as *quickly* tells HOW Paul ran, *hesitantly* tells HOW Charlie tasted the soup—*hesitantly*. These adverbs answer the question, How was the action performed? Such adverbs are called "manner" adverbs because they tell the manner in which an action was performed.

Many manner adverbs are formed by adding *ly* to a corresponding adjective. To illustrate this, let us begin with the adjective *skillful*. In the following sentence, the adjective *skillful* modifies the noun *surgeon*.

Dr. Wilson is a *skillful* surgeon.
↗   ↖
adjective   noun

38

In the next sentence, the adjective *skillful* modifies the noun *manner*.

Dr. Wilson replaces arteries in a *skillful* manner.

                  adjective   noun

But in the following sentence, the adverb *skillfully* modifies the verb *replaced*.

Dr. Wilson *skillfully* replaced the diseased artery.

               adverb   verb

Notice that the adverb *skillfully* is formed by adding *ly* to the adjective *skillful*. In each of the following exercises, you will form an adverb from an adjective and then add the adverb right before the verb in a sentence.

Sample Exercise

Form an adverb by adding *ly* to the underlined adjective in the first sentence. Then rewrite the second sentence with this adverb inserted before the verb *lifted*.

The fireman lifted the child in a <u>careful</u> manner.
The fireman lifted the frightened child from the drain pipe.

Answer Explanation

Step 1. An adverb is formed by adding *ly* to *careful*: *carefully*.

Step 2. The second sentence is written with this adverb inserted before the verb:

The fireman *carefully* lifted the frightened child from the drain pipe.

After students complete several more exercises, they are shown that manner adverbs can often be placed in more than one position. They are told:

In the following sentence, the adverb *hesitantly* is placed before the verb *tasted*.

Charlie *hesitantly* tasted the turtle soup.

However, many adverbs can often be moved to several positions in a sentence. Recall that many sentences have three basic parts: a subject, a verb, and an object.

Charlie tasted the turtle soup.

subject   verb   object

39

A manner adverb often fits well after the object.

Charlie tasted the turtle soup *hesitantly*.

Exercise

Rewrite this sentence with the adverb *suspiciously* moved after the object *squid*.

Our cat suspiciously sniffed the fried squid.

Such exercises not only show students two major positions for manner adverbs. They also reinforce students' familiarity with the three basic parts of many sentences: subject, verb, and object.

Next, students are introduced to adverbs that modify adjectives and other adverbs. They are told:

Some adverbs do not modify verbs. Instead, they modify adjectives or other adverbs. Many of these adverbs are called *intensifiers* because they indicate the intensity or degree of the characteristic referred to by an adjective or adverb. *Very* is an intensifier in the next sentence.

The campers were *very* tired after being kept awake all night.

The adverb *very* modifies the adjective *tired*. In the following sentence, the adverb *quite* modifies the same adjective (*tired*).

The boys were *quite* tired after chopping the wood.

A person who is "very" tired is more tired than a person who is just "quite" tired. Thus, these adverbs (*very*, *quite*) express the degree of the characteristic named by the adjective *tired*.

The next sentence shows an intensifier (*somewhat*) modifying a manner adverb (*recklessly*).

Bill drives *somewhat* recklessly when he is late.

An intensifier is almost always placed right before the adjective or adverb it modifies. In the following exercises, you will add intensifiers to sentences.

Exercise

Rewrite this sentence with *slightly* inserted before *warm*.

The pancakes were just warm when they arrived at the table, so we asked the waiter to bring us fresh hot pancakes.

While most manner adverbs end in *ly*, most intensifiers do not (e.g., *very, quite, somewhat*). Even those that do end in *ly* have a different meaning than manner adverbs. *Slightly* in the above exercise does not mean "in a slight manner" but "to a slight degree." Therefore, putting intensifiers in the same grammatical category as manner adverbs is of questionable value. The main reason that intensifiers are called adverbs is that traditional grammar insists there are only eight parts of speech, and intensifiers do not fit into any other category. In fact, a number of contemporary linguists refer to adverbs as the grammatical dustbin or the catchall category. The *Cambridge Encyclopedia of Language* observes:

> **Several of the traditional parts of speech lacked the coherence required of a well-defined word class—notably the adverb. Some have likened this class to a dustbin, into which grammarians would place any word whose grammatical status was unclear.**

With this qualification in mind, let us now turn to other types of words called adverbs. Words that answer the questions When? Where? How? and How long? are traditionally called adverbs. For example, *yesterday* is an adverb in the next sentence.

We visited two museums *yesterday*.

Traditional grammar textbooks often give students several such examples and then ask them to complete exercises in which they must underline the adverb in a sentence and draw an arrow to the verb it modifies, as in this example.

Unfortunately, Bill failed the math test.

This exercise is based on the traditional definition that adverbs modify verbs, adjectives, or other adverbs. Since *unfortunately* is not modifying an adjective or adverb, it must be modifying a verb. But is *unfortunately* really modifying the verb? It does not seem to be providing more information about the action the way *quickly* does about *ran* in the next sentence.

Jack ran *quickly* down the stairs.

Manner adverbs like *quickly* do modify verbs. They tell how the action was performed. But modern grammarians question whether adverbs like *unfortunately* should be regarded as modifying verbs. One of the leading contemporary grammarians, Sidney Greenbaum, says an adverb like *unfortunately* is an "evaluation of what the sentence refers to." It is a comment on the situation by the writer, an expression of opinion. In short, despite the fact that the term 'adverb" (ad-verb) suggests that adverbs add information to verbs, modern linguists maintain that many of the words called adverbs do not modify verbs. Instead, they are basic sentence elements which contribute various types of information to a sentence.

The P-C Approach avoids the controversial practice of telling students that certain kinds of adverbs modify verbs. Instead, it presents explanations and examples for the types of information that these adverbs provide, and then it asks students to add such adverbs to sentences. Here are some sample explanations and exercises.

Adverbs may add various types of information to a sentence. Here are four types of information contributed by adverbs.

Time: An adverb may tell when an event occurred. The adverb *tonight* provides information about time in this sentence.

We are going to a movie *tonight*.

Place: An adverb may tell where an event occurred, as *outside* does in this sentence.

Dad sometimes exercises *outside* when the weather is nice.

Frequency: An adverb may tell how often an event occurs. *Sometimes* is an adverb in this sentence.

Dad *sometimes* exercises outside when the weather is nice.

Commentary: An adverb may provide a comment (conclusion or opinion) by the writer on the idea expressed in a sentence. *Unfortunately* expresses the writer's opinion about the situation described in this sentence.

Unfortunately, Jack lost the concert tickets.

Exercise

Here are four adverbs.

apparently   upstairs   recently   usually

Each sentence below contains a space indicating a type of adverb. Rewrite each sentence with the appropriate adverb from the four above. Use each adverb only once.

1. The battery was replaced <u>adverb/time</u>, so the car should start easily.

2. Uncle Gilbert hid the toys <u>adverb/place</u>.

3. Having a cavity filled by a dentist is <u>adverb/frequency</u> painless.

4. <u>Adverb/comment</u>, Jim did not study enough to pass his courses.

Modern linguists regard adverbs as a heterogeneous grammatical category, including many different types of words. In fact, work is underway to divide this category into a number of more meaningful groupings, some of which have been tentatively named adjuncts, conjuncts, disjuncts, and subjuncts. Until theoretical grammarians complete the development of such a system, the P-C Approach must be content to show students the different types of adverbs, and then let students practice using them in sentences. After students at an inner-city junior high school spent part of the school year using a workbook developed by Whimbey and Linden, in which grammatical structures are added to sentences, the principal of the school, Vera White, made the following observation:

> **In learning to walk, children need a physical object to hold onto for support. Similarly, in learning to write well, students need a structure for support. This program provides that structure. We like it very much.**

CHAPTER
8

PREPOSITIONS

What is wrong with this advertisement?

> For sale: 1990 Plymouth by an elderly gentleman with a new battery and exhaust system.

The advertisement seems to say that the elderly gentleman has a new battery and exhaust system. Moving the phrase *by an elderly gentleman* eliminates the problem.

> For sale by an elderly gentleman: 1990 Plymouth with a new battery and exhaust system.

The phrase *by an elderly gentleman* is called a *prepositional phrase*. The phrase *with a new battery and exhaust system* is also a prepositional phrase.

This chapter discusses how the P-C Approach teaches prepositional phrases. Here is the introduction presented to students.

> Prepositions are words such as *in*, *on*, *at*, *by*, and *with*. A preposition is generally followed by a noun. The preposition *in* is followed by the noun *garage* in this phrase.

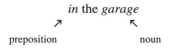

> A phrase consisting of a preposition followed by a noun is called a prepositional phrase. The noun is called the object of the preposition.

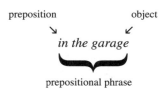

> A preposition is used to express the relationship between its object and some other part of a sentence. Consider this sentence.

> > The car *in the garage* belongs to Anita.

> The preposition *in* expresses the relationship between the *garage* and the *car*, namely, that the car is physically within the garage.

> Some prepositions, such as *in* and *on*, express simple spatial relationships. Other prepositions, such as *from* and *despite*, represent other types of relationships, as illustrated by this exercise.

Exercise

> Here are two prepositional phrases.

> > from the children   despite the rain

> Below are two sentences. Rewrite each sentence with one of the above prepositional phrases in the position indicated.

> > 1. The baseball game continued <u>PREPOSITIONAL PHRASE</u>.

> > 2. Jack hid the candy <u>PREPOSITIONAL PHRASE</u>.

Students are then shown that prepositional phrases can be used to modify nouns:

> Compare these sentences.

> > The car <u>in the garage</u> needs a tune-up.
> > The car <u>in the driveway</u> is running perfectly.

Notice that the underlined prepositional phrases help identify the cars. They provide more information about the cars. Therefore, these prepositional phrases are said to modify the noun *car*. In the following exercise, you will modify a noun with a prepositional phrase.

Sample Exercise

Rewrite the first sentence with the underlined prepositional phrase from the second sentence inserted right after the noun it modifies.

> The sherbet belongs to Sarah.
> The sherbet is <u>in the refrigerator</u>.

Answer Explanation

The prepositional phrase provides information about the sherbet. Therefore, it is inserted right after the noun *sherbet*.

> The sherbet *in the refrigerator* belongs to Sarah.

After completing several exercises, students are given another opportunity to see prepositional phrases modifying nouns by moving misplaced prepositional phrases:

> Can you see what is wrong with this sentence?
>
> A waitress brought my turkey sandwich with a grumpy attitude.
>
> The prepositional phrase *with a grumpy attitude* is misplaced. The sentence seems to say that the sandwich had a grumpy attitude. But the writer probably meant to say that the waitress had a grumpy attitude. Rewrite the sentence with the prepositional phrase moved so that it is right after the noun it should modify.

Next students are shown that prepositional phrases can serve other functions besides modifying nouns:

> Some prepositional phrases do not modify nouns. Instead, they present additional information about an action or event described in a sentence. The prepositional phrase *after lunch* tells when the family went skiing.
>
> The whole family went skiing *after lunch*.

There are many prepositions, and they provide various types of information. A list of prepositions is presented to students, but many students just skim over the list and forget most of it quickly. Therefore, the P-C Approach presents a large array of prepositional phrases to students in the context of using them for adding information to sentences. Students are shown that some prepositional phrases can be placed at several positions in a sentence:

> When a prepositional phrase presents information about a noun, it is generally placed right after the noun. But when a prepositional phrase presents information about the time or location of an event, it can often be placed at different positions in a sentence with little or no change in meaning. Here is a sentence with a prepositional phrase at the end.

> I generally gain five or six pounds *during the Christmas season.*

> This prepositional phrase could also be placed at the beginning of the sentence.

> *During the Christmas season*, I generally gain five or six pounds.
>
> ↗
>
> comma

> Notice that a prepositional phrase at the beginning of a sentence is often set off with a comma so that it is easier for a reader to see where the rest of the sentence begins.

Exercises

1. Rewrite this sentence with the underlined prepositional phrase moved to the front and set off with one comma.

   I wish, <u>at times like this</u>, that I had graduated from college.

2. Short prepositional phrases are often not set off with commas. Rewrite this sentence with *in my heart* moved to the beginning and with *in my mind* moved right after *but*. Do not add any commas.

   I wish them well *in my heart*, but I question their judgment *in my mind.*

Next students are shown that many sentences contain several prepositional phrases providing different types of information:

> The following sentence contains two prepositional phrases.

> Bob went *to the store for some ice cream.*

> The prepositional phrase *to the store* tells Bob's destination. The prepositional phrase *for some ice cream* explains the purpose of his action.

Exercises

1. Here are three prepositional phrases, labeled A, B, and C.

   A. about the factors
   B. to the Civil War
   C. on my desk

   Rewrite the following sentence with the above prepositional phrases inserted in the positions indicated by the letters.

   The book <u>A</u> leading <u>B</u> is <u>C</u> .

2. Here are two prepositional phrases, one beginning with the preposition *despite* and the other beginning with the preposition *at*.

   despite her admitted nervousness

   at her graduation ceremony

   Rewrite this sentence with the prepositional phrases in the positions shown. Place a comma after the first prepositional phrase but not after the second because it is more closely related to what follows.

   Despite phrase, at phrase my sister delivered an inspiring speech to the graduating seniors and their guests.

Students are also shown how to use a prepositional phrase for modifying the object of a previous prepositional phrase:

   The underlined prepositional phrase in the next sentence tells where the event occurred.

   We negotiated the contract <u>by the pool</u>.

The prepositional phrase in the following sentence tells where the pool is located.

   The pool is *at the Riviera Hotel.*

This prepositional phrase can be added to the first sentence.

   We negotiated the contract by the pool *at the Riviera Hotel.*

Note that *at the Riviera Hotel* modifies the noun *pool.* Thus, the second prepositional phrase modifies the object of the first prepositional phrase. We can even modify the second object (*Riviera Hotel*) with a third prepositional phrase, based on the information in the next sentence.

   The Riviera Hotel is *in Las Vegas, Nevada.*

   We negotiated the contract by the pool at the Riviera Hotel *in Las Vegas, Nevada.*

Thus we see that useful details can be added to a sentence by letting prepositional phrases modify the objects of other prepositional phrases.

Exercises

1. Rewrite the first sentence with the prepositional phrases from the other sentences.

   Jack broke his leg falling.
   The fall was *off the stage*.
   The stage is *in the auditorium*.
   The auditorium is *at our school*.

2. Rewrite the first sentence with the prepositional phrase from the second sentence inserted after the noun it modifies.

   Jack put the money in the vase and went to bed.
   The vase is *on the refrigerator*.

A common cause of subject-verb agreement errors is illustrated by the following sentence.

> Wrong: The theme of all the speeches *were* that success
> requires dedication.

The subject of the sentence (*theme*) is singular, and therefore the verb should also be singular (*was*). However, a prepositional phrase intervenes between the subject and verb, and its object is plural (*speeches*). Because this plural noun is closer to the verb than the subject, inexperienced writers sometimes use a plural verb in such a sentence. To show students that the form of a verb should agree with the subject, even when a prepositional phrase intervenes between the subject and verb, students complete exercises in which they insert prepositional phrases modifying subjects. They are told:

> Sometimes a prepositional phrase modifies the subject of a sentence, as illustrated in the following exercises.

Exercises

In each exercise, rewrite the first sentence with the prepositional phrase from the second sentence inserted after the noun it modifies.

1. Money is included in the governor's budget.
   The money is *for new textbooks and computers*.

2. The trees look strong and healthy.
   The trees are *around the lake*.

Having students insert prepositional phrases between subjects and verbs helps them avoid subject-verb agreement errors because they clearly see the subject and verb before the prepositional phrase is inserted. To ensure that students fully understand this construction, it is explained and reinforced with another set of exercises:

Here is the answer for one of the above exercises.

Money for new textbooks and computers *is* included in the governor's budget.

Note that the verb in the sentence (*is*) is singular because the subject (*money*) is singular. When a prepositional phrase with a plural object, such as *new textbooks and computers*, intervenes between a singular subject and verb, some inexperienced writers become confused and use a plural verb.

Wrong: Money for new textbooks and computers *are* included in the governor's budget.

To avoid this type of error, remember that an intervening prepositional phrase does not affect the verb. The verb must agree with the subject.

Exercises

In each of the following sentences, one or more prepositional phrases intervene between the subject and the verb. Determine whether the subject is singular or plural. Then write the sentence with the correct verb.

1. The letters to the editor in my local newspaper is/are often very funny.

2. Paris, with its luxurious hotels, excellent restaurants, and outstanding museums, attract/attracts many tourists in the summer.

In exercises such as the last one, students are asked to write the entire sentence rather than just underline the correct verb because such writing can improve an array of writing skills, ranging from the correct spelling of particular words and a reduction in subject-verb agreement errors to the use of advanced sentence patterns. For example, a student who has never written the word *luxurious* before may be more likely to include the word in his own future writing. Copying *museum* may improve his ability to spell this word. James Jones, the author of *From Here to Eternity*, revealed to his biographer (MacShane) that as an exercise to improve his own writing skills he copied the prose of other fine writers because he discovered that "one could read until one's eyes are red, but only by copying word for word could one see how a writer builds up his effect." Copying the above sentence, with its compound prepositional phrase set off with commas and placed between the subject and verb, helps students internalize a pattern that they can use to express their own ideas in writing. In our multi-cultural society, with many students coming from homes in which standard English is not the primary language, the immersion in standard written English that results from having students copy entire sentences in P-C exercises is an invaluable experience for improving confidence and competence in writing.

CHAPTER

9

CREATING COMPOUND STRUCTURES WITH COORDINATING CONJUNCTIONS

I n an article presenting a number of reasons for teaching grammar more effectively in our schools, Professor Bill McCleary reported in *Composition Chronicle* that: "every college writing teacher can attest that the only 'rule' which every freshman can cite is the completely false one about never beginning a sentence with a coordinating conjunction." In other words, under the current system of teaching grammar, one of the main bits of grammatical knowledge that many students bring with them to college is erroneous. We will come back to this erroneous notion shortly. But first let us look at some correct uses of coordinating conjunctions. Here is how we introduce them to students.

Conjunctions are words used to join sentences or parts of sentences. For example, here are two simple sentences.

> Joe washes the dishes.
> Carla puts them away.

These sentences can be joined with the conjunction *and*.

> Joe washes the dishes, *and* Carla puts them away.
> ↑
> conjunction

There are several types of conjunctions. This chapter discusses coordinating conjunctions. Another type of conjunction is discussed in a later chapter.

Coordinating conjunctions form the smallest class of conjunctions, with only seven words in this grammatical group: *and*, *or*, *but*, *so*, *for*, *yet*, and *nor*. Conjunctions do more than just join sentences or parts of sentences. They also express relationships between ideas. Here are some relationships expressed by the coordinating conjunctions.

AND signals that a similar idea is being added to the previous one.

OR introduces an alternative.

BUT introduces a contrasting idea.

SO introduces a result.

FOR introduces a reason.

YET introduces a strongly contrasting idea.

NOR joins two negative ideas.

In joining two sentences with a coordinating conjunction, the conjunction is placed between the sentences. Also, a comma is generally placed before the conjunction:

> Francine brought the sandwiches, *but* Frank forgot the sodas.
> ↖
> comma

In each of the following exercises, you will be presented with two sentences and two conjunctions. Decide which conjunction expresses the relationship between the sentences. Then write the sentences joined with that conjunction. Try this sample exercise.

Sample Exercise

Write these sentences joined with *or* or *but*.

> The family was poor.
> The children still managed to receive a good education.

Answer Explanation

The sentences present two contrasting ideas, not alternatives. Therefore, they can be joined with *but*.

> The family was poor, *but* the children still managed to receive a good education.   ↖
> > comma

After completing a number of similar exercises, students are shown how *and* can be used to join two sentences with different subjects but identical predicates. First several terms are explained:

> In discussing parts of sentences, it is useful to understand the following terms: *predicate*, *simple subject,* and *complete subject.* In a sentence of the following type, everything except the subject is called the *predicate.*

> The salesman is retiring next year

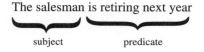

> > subject   predicate

> If the subject is modified by adjectives and prepositional phrases, they are considered part of the complete subject.

> The best salesman on the West Coast is retiring next year.

> > complete subject   predicate

> The main noun in a subject is called the "simple subject." The simple subject along with its modifiers is called the "complete subject." In the above sentence, the simple subject is *salesman.* The complete subject is *the best salesman on the West Coast.*

> If two sentences have different subjects but identical predicates, sometimes the subjects can be joined with *and.* Here are two such sentences.

> > The best salesman on the West Coast is retiring next year.
> > The manager of the New York office is retiring next year.

> Here is how the sentences can be combined:

> > The best salesman on the West Coast *and* the manager of the New York office are retiring next year. ↖
> > > conjunction

> Note several points about the last sentence. First, the complete subjects rather than just the simple subjects are included in the combined sentence.

You could join just the simple subjects like this:

The salesman *and* the manager are retiring next year.

However, joining just the simple subject omits useful information.

Note also that the verbs in the separate sentences are singular. But the verb in the combined sentence is plural.

The best salesman on the West Coast *is* retiring next year.

↖

singular verb

The manager of the New York office *is* retiring next year.

↖

singular verb

The best salesman on the West Coast and the manager of the New York office *are* retiring next year.

↖

plural verb

A combination of two subjects joined by *and* is called a "compound subject."

conjunction
↙
The best salesman on the West Coast *and* the manager of the New York office .

compound subject

A compound subject is plural and requires a plural verb.

Finally, notice that there is no comma before the conjunction *and*.

The best salesman on the West Coast *and* the manager of the New York office are retiring next year.   ↖

no comma

When just parts of sentences are joined with a conjunction, a comma is generally not used. A comma is needed only when complete sentences are joined.

Exercise

Rewrite these sentences as a single sentence with a compound subject.

A small bowl of vegetable soup is all I want for dinner tonight.
A few saltine crackers with cheese are all I want for dinner tonight.

Many traditional grammar textbooks try to define the terms *simple subject* and *complete subject* early in the course—before teaching adjectives and prepositional phrases—and then ask students to identify the simple and complete subjects in a group of sentences. This practice is based on the beliefs that sentence subjects are more fundamental concepts than modifiers, and that students should understand simple and complete subjects intuitively from using the language. However, the fact that students understand them intuitively does not mean that they understand them formally with grammatical terms and analyzed parts. Students recognize complete subjects more readily after they have modified simple subjects with adjectives and prepositional phrases. Furthermore, the concept of a complete subject is more functionally meaningful after students have combined complete subjects from pairs of sentences to form compound subjects. This is just one example of how the P-C Approach gives students more meaningful experiences with grammatical concepts than the traditional approach does in having students just label parts of sentences with grammatical terms.

Students are next shown how to use AND for joining other elements in sentences:

> Sentences whose subjects are identical but whose predicates are partly or completely different can sometimes be joined with *and*. Here are two sentences whose predicates are partly different.

> > Maria has a larger office in her new job.
> > Maria has a higher salary in her new job.

Let us examine the grammatical parts of these sentences.

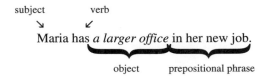

Both sentences have the same subject, verb, and prepositional phrase. They differ in their objects. To combine the sentences, the identical parts can be written just once, and the parts that are different are joined with *and*.

Maria has *a larger office and higher salary* in her new job.

compound object

A combination of two objects joined by *and* is called a "compound object."

Singular common nouns are often preceded by the little words *a*, *an*, or *the*. These three words form a special grammatical class called "articles." The objects in both of the original sentences are preceded by *a* (*a* larger office, *a* higher salary). In combining sentences, you can sometimes emphasize the different parts more strongly by repeating the articles. Also, the combined sentence may sound better by repeating the articles. Which of these sentences do you prefer?

> Maria has *a* larger office and higher salary in her new job.
> Maria has *a* larger office and *a* higher salary in her new job.

In general, when you combine sentences, you may repeat any words to improve the sound or meaning of the final sentence.

Exercises

Rewrite each pair of sentences as a single sentence with the parts that are different joined by *and*.

1. The safe contained all the money I owned.
    The safe contained all the jewelry I owned.

2. Every Saturday Phil washes his new Mustang convertible.
    Every Saturday Phil waxes his new Mustang convertible.

Students are next shown how other coordinating conjunctions can be used to join parts of sentence. They complete exercises of the following type.

Exercises

1. Rewrite these sentences as a single sentence with the parts that are different joined by *yet*.

    Our dinner was absolutely delicious.
    Our dinner was surprisingly inexpensive.

2. Rewrite these sentences as a single sentence with the parts that are different joined by *but*.

    Harry woke up an hour late this morning.
    Harry went to work anyway.

3. Rewrite these sentences as a single sentence with the parts that are different joined by *or*.

   A steak can be cooked in a frying pan.
   A steak can be cooked over the open flame of a barbecue grill.

4. Rewrite these sentences as a single sentence with the parts that are different joined by *or*.

   Jack hid the front door key under the door mat.
   Jack hid the front door key in the flower pot at the corner of the house.

By the time students have reached this point in the chapter, they will have analyzed about two dozen pairs of sentences and combined them with coordinating conjunctions. Extending the process to combine three or more sentences is now an easy step for them to take. They are told:

Coordinating conjunctions can also be used to combine three or more whole sentences or parts of sentences. Here are three sentences with identical subjects (*Joe's car*) and verbs (*is*), but different adjectives.

   Joe's car is old.
   Joe's car is noisy.
   Joe's car is unreliable.

These three sentences can be combined with the conjunction *and* in this way.

conjunction
↙
Joe's car is old, noisy, and unreliable.
↖   ↗
commas

Note that there is a comma between the first and second adjectives. Note also that the second adjective is followed by another comma and then the conjunction *and*. This example shows the most common pattern for combining three or more sentences or parts of sentences with a coordinating conjunction. A comma is placed between each element, and the last element is preceded by the conjunction.

Three whole sentences can even be combined in this pattern. Here are three sentences.

   Denise is on the tennis team.
   Judy is in the school jazz band.
   Sarah may join the drama club.

These three sentences are short, and if they were written separately in a letter or an article, they would seem choppy and immature. They can be combined with two commas and the conjunction *and*.

comma   comma
↓   ↓

  Denise is on the tennis team, Judy is in the school jazz band, and Sarah may join the drama club.   ↗

conjunction

Magazines and newspapers often omit the second comma in a series of three items. For example, here is the sentence about Joe's car with the second comma omitted.

  Joe's car was old, noisy and unreliable.

↖

comma omitted

However, in business and academic writing, a comma is generally included before the conjunction. Include this comma in the following exercises.

Exercises

1. Rewrite these sentences as a single sentence using the conjunction *and*. Remember to make the verb plural.

   A balanced diet is necessary for good health.
   Sensible exercise is necessary for good health.
   Adequate rest is necessary for good health.

2. Rewrite these four sentences as a single sentence using the conjunction *and*.

   Mr. Garcia has wavy black hair.
   Mr. Garcia has a small moustache.
   Mr. Garcia has a warm smile.
   Mr. Garcia has a sincere commitment to help students become better writers.

3. Rewrite these sentences as a single sentence using the conjunction *or*.

   The battery connections on your car may be loose.
   The starter may be broken.
   The ignition switch may be worn.

4. Rewrite these sentences as a single sentence using the conjunction *or*.

   The students labeled each clause an adverb clause.
   The students labeled each clause an adjective clause.
   The students labeled each clause a noun clause.

The final topic that we deal with concerns the erroneous information mentioned in the quotation from Professor McCleary reprinted at the beginning of this chapter: Can a sentence begin with a coordinating conjunction? We assure students that starting a sentence with a coordinating conjunction is grammatically fine, and we explain why a writer might occasionally want to do so:

> Students sometimes ask whether it is all right to begin a sentence with a coordinating conjunction. Yes, it is. On almost every page of quality publications such as *Newsweek* and *Time*, you will find sentences beginning with *but*, *or*, *and*, or *yet*. One reason for beginning with a coordinating conjunction is to make a long sentence more readable. For example, below is a long sentence containing the coordinating conjunction *but*. Rewrite this sentence as two sentences by letting *but* begin the second sentence.
>
> > A novelist, like a reporter, must look at a situation carefully, observe what people are doing, and listen to what they are saying, but in the case of the novelist, the setting, the dialogue, and the action are all occurring inside his or her head, born of experience, emotion, and imagination.
>
> If you have just written the above sentence as two sentences, you can see that starting the second sentence with *but* signals a reader that the second sentence presents information which contrasts with the ideas of the first sentence. This is the same role that *but* plays in the original long sentence. However, since the original sentence is somewhat complicated, containing a series of three predicates connected with commas and *and*, as well as three subjects connected with commas and *and*, separating it into two sentences presents a less dense and formidable picture to readers.
>
> Another reason for starting a sentence with a coordinating conjunction is to catch the reader's attention and make a point strongly. For example, in a *U.S. News and World Report* article entitled "Tax Cuts," the first paragraph states that several leading economists believe President Bush's tax cuts will stimulate America's economy. The second paragraph opens with the following sentence: "But hold on." This short sentence is very effective for signaling the reader that the writer is not totally convinced by these economic gurus—that he is about to shift gears and present the other side of the story. So begin your sentences with coordinating conjunctions whenever you think the result is an effective sentence, as we did in starting this sentence with *so*.

CHAPTER

10

PRONOUNS

The word *pronoun* consists of the prefix *pro* and the root *noun*. In this context, the prefix *pro* means "taking the place of." Thus, the word pronoun means literally "taking the place of a noun." Pronouns are, in fact, words that can play *the* same roles in sentences that nouns can play—subject, object, etc.

Students have difficulty with pronouns for two reasons: 1. Pronouns are somewhat complicated; and 2. Using pronouns correctly requires understanding other grammatical concepts, namely, subjects, objects, and prepositions. There are seven types of pronouns. Let us begin by looking at how the P-C Approach introduces students to the most common type of pronoun: personal pronouns.

Personal pronouns are words such as *he*, *she*, *they*, and *it*. Personal pronouns can replace nouns in a sentence. For example, *Deana* is the subject in both of these sentence.

Deana wants to be a concert pianist.
Deana practices every day.

To avoid repeating *Deana* in the second sentence, the personal pronoun *she* can be used.

Deana wants to be a concert pianist. *She* practices every day.

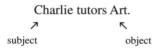

personal pronoun

Most personal pronouns have one form to use as a subject in a sentence and a different form to use as an object. Recall from Chapter 3 that a basic sentence has a subject, a verb, and an object.

Charlie tutors Art.

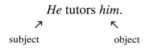

subject   object

Note what happens when you replace the names in the above sentence with pronouns.

He tutors *him*.

subject   object

Charlie is replaced by *he* because *Charlie* is the subject in the sentence. But *Art* is replaced by *him* because *Art* is the object.

Here are the subject and object forms for the personal pronouns.

Subject Form	Object Form
I	me
you	you
we	us
he	him
she	her
it	it
they	them

When this chart is presented in a traditional grammar class, students begin to look at the teacher with blank stares. Most students are not on friendly terms with *subject* and *object*. In an article in *English Journal*, a major publication from the National Council of Teachers of English. Professor Ed Varva writes: "The fact is, most students cannot identify the subjects and verbs in their own writing." In another article in the same journal, Professors Stephen Tchudi and Lee Thomas make the following observation about their university students: "we found that most of our students *had* been taught traditional grammar once if not several times. The trouble was, the teaching hadn't stuck and had mainly succeeded in making students self-conscious about their 'grammar'..."

In contrast, students who have worked through the previous chapters in our P-C workbook do have a functional understanding of subjects, verbs, and objects. They have manipulated and modified subjects. They have also combined objects from different sentences with coordinating conjunctions. Therefore, the above chart presents meaningful information that they can use.

After students examine the chart, they are told:

> Notice in the above chart that only *you* and *it* have the same form for the subject and object in a sentence. The other pronouns have different subject and object forms.

> People generally use single pronouns correctly. But inexperienced writers can make errors with compound subjects or objects. For instance, what is wrong with this sentence?

> > Wrong: Mr. Philips picked Vanessa and I for the track team.

> The pronoun (*I*) is part of the compound object.

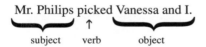

> Therefore, the object form (*me*) should be used.

> > Correct: Mr. Philips picked Vanessa and *me* for the track team.

> There are two ways to decide which pronoun to use in a compound structure.

> Method 1: Analyze the sentence grammatically to determine whether the compound structure is the subject or the object. We illustrated this method in the above example.

> Method 2: Cross out the other words in the compound structure so that only the pronoun is left.

> Here are the above sentences with *Vanessa and* crossed out.

> > Mr. Philips picked ~~Vanessa and~~ I for the track team.

> > Mr. Philips picked ~~Vanessa and~~ me for the track team.

Your ear probably tells you that "Mr. Philips picked I" sounds wrong. It tells you that "Mr. Philips picked me" is correct. Therefore, you know that the pronoun in the compound structure should be *me*.

In each of the following exercises, you will rewrite a sentence with the correct pronoun. Try this sample exercise.

Sample Exercise

In the sentence below, you are offered a choice of pronouns. Rewrite the sentence with the correct pronoun.

> Judy and <u>I/me</u> enrolled in an architecture class.

Answer Explanation

The pronoun is part of the subject of the sentence.

> Judy and <u>I/me</u> enrolled in an architecture class.

Compound Subject

The table presented earlier shows that the subject form of *I/me* is *I*. Therefore *Judy and I* is correct.

> Judy and *I* enrolled in an architecture class.

Another way to find the answer is to cross out *Judy and*.

> ~~Judy and~~ <u>I/me</u> enrolled in an architecture class.

Your "ear for English" tells you that *I* is correct.

> Correct: I enrolled in an architecture class.
> Wrong: Me enrolled in an architecture class.

Therefore, the compound subject is *Judy and I*.

> Judy and *I* enrolled in an architecture class.

Exercises

The following sentences offer you a choice of pronouns. Rewrite each sentence with the correct pronoun.

1. The company gave Al and <u>I/me</u> computers as prizes for our perfect attendance records.
2. Al and <u>I/me</u> received computers from the company.
3. The Smiths and <u>we/us</u> arrived at the party late.
4. Paul did not recognize Jim and <u>I/me</u> in our costumes.

Students are next shown that the object form of a pronoun should be used when the pronoun is the object of a preposition. They are told:

> When the object of a preposition is a pronoun, the object form of the pronoun should be used. For example, in the following sentence the preposition *with* is followed by a pronoun. Do you think the correct pronoun is *I* or *me*?
>
> With <u>I/me</u> helping, the roof was repaired in just one day.
>
> Since the pronoun is the object of the preposition *with*, the object form (*me*) must be used.
>
> With *me* helping, the roof was repaired in just one day.
>
> People seldom make mistakes when the object of a preposition is just a single pronoun. But inexperienced writers often make mistakes when a preposition has a compound object, and when a pronoun is part of that compound structure. For example, inexperienced writers might incorrectly use the pronoun *I* instead of *me* in the following sentence.
>
> Wrong: With Bob and *I* helping, the roof was repaired in just one day.
>
> Right: With Bob and *me* helping, the roof was repaired in just one day.

One reason the P-C Approach teaches prepositions before pronouns is that pronouns are more complicated than prepositions. Another reason is that it allows us to discuss the correct pronoun case when a pronoun is the object of a preposition. However, many traditional grammarians teach pronouns before prepositions. They place the pronoun chapter near the beginning of the text—right after nouns—because they are primarily concerned with grammar rather than pedagogy: They reason that since pronouns can replace nouns in a sentence, pronouns are closely related to nouns and should be taught right after nouns. The result is that when traditional grammarians try to teach students to use the appropriate form of a pronoun after a preposition, most students have only a vague idea of what the term "object of a preposition" means. The lesson falls on unprepared ears.

Incidentally, linguists attribute the following type of mistake to two sources.

> Wrong: With Bob and *I* helping, the roof was repaired in just one day.

First, the prepositional phrase is near the beginning of the sentence. This is "subject territory." In other words, people are accustomed to hearing *I* rather than *me* before the verb of a sentence. We say "I would like more gravy," not "Me would like more gravy." Because the pronoun is in subject territory, *I* sounds right.

The second source of the error is what linguists call "hypercorrection" or "overcorrection." Children have been told repeatedly and vigorously that *me* is wrong in the following type of sentence.

Wrong: Bob and *me* went to the movie.

Instead, *I* must be used.

Correct: Bob and *I* went to the movie.

As a result, people come to think that *Bob and I* sounds more polite or more educated, and they write sentences such as this:

Uncle Hector sent those books to Bob and I.

In the last sentence, the pronoun *I* is part of the compound object of the preposition *to*. Therefore, *me* should be used.

Uncle Hector sent those books to Bob and *me*.

Overcorrection is an example of what psychologists call overgeneralization of a response, and overgeneralization tends to occur when a person cannot discriminate the appropriate stimulus for a response from an inappropriate stimulus. Many students do not understand prepositions. In fact, many do not even understand subjects fully. Therefore, they are not able to effectively discriminate the grammatical difference between these sentences.

Between you and me, Jack is being foolish.
You and I think that Jack is being foolish.

If students do not understand that in the first sentence, *me* is part of the prepositional phrase which precedes the subject *Jack*, whereas in the second sentence *I* is part of the compound subject, they will not understand why *I* would be incorrect in the first sentence.

Wrong: Between you and *I*, Jack is being foolish.

The traditional approach leaves many students with an inadequate grasp of grammar, so they cannot see that *me* should be used in the last sentence.

The P-C Approach recognizes that students may not have learned the entire list of prepositions presented in the prepositions chapter. Therefore, the preposition is identified in each of the following exercises. The exercises, thus, provide practice not only in choosing the correct pronoun but also in recognizing various prepositions. Here is a sample exercise.

Sample Exercise

Rewrite this sentence with the correct pronoun in the compound object of the preposition *between*.

> Between you and I/me, Bill does not know how to barbecue a steak properly.

Answer Explanation

The subject of this sentence is *Bill*. The phrase *between you and I/me* is a prepositional phrase in front of the subject. Since the pronoun is in the compound object of the preposition, the correct form is *me*.

> Between you and *me*, Bill does not know how to barbecue a steak properly.

Exercises

In each sentence a preposition is underlined, and you are offered a choice of pronouns in the compound object of that preposition. Rewrite the sentence with the correct pronoun.

1. A rich lady left all her money to her cat and I/me.
2. *Between* you and I/me, the food was terrible.
3. *Besides* you and she/her, who else from the company is attending the conference?

After students have completed a number of exercises, the workbook turns to another problem that can occur with pronouns: ambiguous reference. First, the advantages and risks of using pronouns are explained:

> Pronouns can be used in the noun slots of sentences, but they are generally less specific than nouns: they can refer to more things. For example, a proper noun like *Empire State Building* is more specific than a common noun like *building*, because *building* can represent any building—the building where you live, the building across the street, or the White House. But *building* is more specific than the corresponding pronoun *it*. *It* can represent not only a building but also a bus, a book, or a beret. This versatility makes pronouns a useful verbal tool. A writer can save the time and space required to write *Empire State Building* again and again by just writing *it*. However, within a particular verbal context, the referent of a pronoun must be clear and specific, or else communication breaks down: The reader must know what the writer is referring to with a pronoun like *it* or *they*. When a reader cannot tell what a pronoun refers to, the writer has made an error called "ambiguous pronoun reference."

> The word that the pronoun replaces or stands for is called its *antecedent*.

What is the antecedent of *they* in this sentence?

> After the mayor and his wife watched the elephants perform, *they* were taken behind the tent and fed several bales of hay.

The antecedent of *they* is undoubtedly *elephants*. However, as you read through the sentence, you might think that *they* refers to the mayor and his wife until you reach "bales of hay." And in a humorous mood, a person might suggest that *they* does refer to a chubby local mayor and his wife. However, a sentence in serious prose should not be open to two interpretations.

In the next sentence, it is impossible to decide what the antecedent of *he* is. In the spaces below the sentence, write the two possible antecedents

> Jack called Fred when *he* was in the hospital.
>
> Antecedent 1:_____
>
> Antecedent 2:_____

Sometimes an ambiguous pronoun can be corrected by replacing it with the intended antecedent. For example, the meanings of the following sentences are no longer ambiguous.

> Jack called Fred when Jack was in the hospital.
> Jack called Fred when Fred was in the hospital.

Exercises

1. Rewrite this sentence with *she* replaced by *Joslin*.

   Joslin and Denise exchanged shifts at work because *she* wanted to attend junior college classes that were offered only during her shift.

2. Rewrite this sentence with *it* replaced by *the missing part*.

   If you find any part missing from one of our outstanding home-assembly furniture kits, let us know by calling our 800 number, and we will send *it* immediately.

Through such exercises, students become aware of the types of ambiguity or weak pronoun reference that can creep into a sentence.

There are seven types of pronouns: personal, reflexive, intensive, demonstrative, indefinite, relative, and interrogative. Relative pronouns are covered in a later chapter on relative clauses, and interrogative pronouns are covered in the chapters on forming noun clauses and forming questions. Reflexive, intensive, demonstrative, and indefinite pronouns, as well as possessive forms of personal pronouns, are taught in the pronoun chapter of the P-C workbook with lessons similar to those shown earlier for correct pronoun usage: the pronouns are discussed, their functions are illustrated, and then students construct sentences using them.

The first sample exercise in this chapter illustrates the strategy of crossing out an element in a compound structure to help determine which pronoun is correct. However, this strategy is not infallible. In our multi-cultural society, with many students coming from homes in which standard English is not the primary language, and with a large number even coming from foreign countries, students cannot trust their "ear for English" in picking the correct pronoun. The only sure way to decide the correct pronoun is through a grammatical analysis of the sentence. But this requires that a student understand subjects, objects, prepositions, and objects of prepositions. Unfortunately, the widely used traditional approach to grammar does not teach these concepts well. Consequently, many of the pronoun errors that students make are actually rooted in their poor understanding of other grammatical concepts. These fundamental concepts must be taught more effectively before students will see that pronoun usage is rational and manageable.

CHAPTER
11

SUBORDINATING CONJUNCTIONS AND COMPLEX SENTENCES

Occasionally school superintendents visit classrooms. On one such occasion, a district superintendent asked a student in a high school English class what a "subordinate clause" is. Without any hesitation, the student answered, "A subordinate clause is subordinate to a clause, like one of Santa Claus' little helpers." Is this a true story? Perhaps. Constance Weaver, one of the leading experts on grammar in the National Council of Teachers of English, writes: "many teachers themselves do not have a solid understanding of the grammatical concepts they try to teach. . . ." So what can we expect of students? With the P-C Approach, much more. Here is how the P-C Approach introduces students to subordinate clauses and subordinating conjunctions.

This chapter discusses subordinating conjunctions and their role in creating a type of highly informative sentence that is indispensable in scientific and technical writing. Subordinating conjunctions are like coordinating conjunctions in allowing you to combine two sentences into one with a word that shows the relationship between the ideas in the sentences. Here is how two sentences can be combined with the subordinating conjunction *because*.

> Paul failed two courses.
> He must take them again in summer school.

subordinating conjunction
↙

Because Paul failed two courses, he must take them again in summer school.   ↖

comma

Note that *because* is placed at the beginning of the combined sentence and that a comma is placed between the original sentences.

The conjunction *because* is used in expressing a cause-effect relationship between two events.

Because *Paul failed two courses, he must take them again in summer school.*

cause   effect or result

Because is placed before the group of words describing the cause. Use this same pattern in the following exercise.

Sample Exercise

Here are two sentences. Decide which one describes the cause and which describes the result. Then rewrite the sentences as one sentence using the pattern shown above.

> We had no water for drinking or washing.
> Our water pipes froze.

Answer Explanation

The second sentence describes the cause. Therefore *because* is placed before the second sentence.

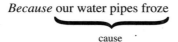

Because our water pipes froze

cause

The first sentence describes the effect or result. To follow the pattern shown above, it must be written after the cause, set off with a comma.

Because our water pipes froze, we had no water for drinking or washing

cause   effect or result

Generally a subordinating conjunction can be placed at either the beginning of the combined sentences or between the original sentences. Here is the answer with *because* placed between the original sentences. Note that *because* still introduces the cause.

We had no water for drinking or washing *because* our water pipes froze

effect   cause

This sentence and the answer for the above exercise show the two main patterns used for sentences with subordinating conjunctions.

Pattern I

> *Because* our water pipes froze, we had no water for drinking or washing.   ↖
>
>   comma

Pattern II

> We had no water for drinking or washing *because* our water pipes froze.

In Pattern I, the subordinating conjunction is placed at the beginning of the combined sentence, and a comma is placed between the original sentences. In Pattern II, the subordinating conjunction is placed between the original sentences, and a comma is not required.

Exercise

Combine these sentences using *because* and Pattern II.

> The air is becoming polluted.
> Some people are have breathing problems.

Answer Explanation

The cause is presented in the first sentence, so *because* is written before it.

> because *the air is becoming polluted*
>
>   cause

In Pattern II, *because* is placed between the original sentences.

Some people are have breathing problems *because* the air is becoming polluted.

A basic term in the field of grammar is "clause." A "clause" consists of a subject and a verb. It may also include other grammatical structures such as objects and modifiers. Here are two clauses.

we conserve water
we will soon have a water shortage

An "independent" clause can stand alone as a sentence. Both of the above clauses are independent clauses and can be written as sentences.

We conserve water.
We will soon have a water shortage.

But a "dependent" clause cannot stand alone. One type of dependent clause contains an extra word that prevents the clause from standing alone. Here is such a dependent clause.

unless we conserve water

The word *unless* prevents this clause from standing alone. If you heard someone say, "unless we conserve water, " you would expect the person to say something else to complete the thought. You would wonder, what will happen unless we conserve water? A dependent clause must be attached to an independent clause to form a complex sentence.

Unless we conserve water, we will soon have a water shortage.

A dependent clause is grammatically "dependent" in the sense that it depends on the independent clause to form a complete sentence.

A combination of a dependent clause and an independent clause is called a "complex sentence."

complex sentence

Unless we conserve water, we will soon have a water shortage.

dependent clause   independent clause

complex sentence

We will soon have a water shortage unless we conserve water.

independent clause   dependent clause

Exercises

1. Create a dependent clause by writing this sentence with the subordinating conjunction *after* in front. Note: A dependent clause does *not* start with a capital letter nor end with a period.

   He failed the first three exams.

2. Write a complex sentence by combining the clauses below with the independent clause first.

   after he failed the first three exams
   Phil dropped his Greek history class

There are only seven coordinating conjunctions. But there are several dozen subordinating conjunctions, giving you more options for combining sentences and expressing relationships. A representative sample of subordinating conjunctions are presented in this chapter. The others are generally used in a similar way. Once you understand the main characteristics of subordinating conjunctions, you can master the others by observing how they are used in the materials that you read.

Students are shown why a comma is generally used when a subordinating conjunction is placed at the beginning of a complex sentence but not when it is placed between the two clauses. They are asked:

Where would a comma be useful in this complex sentence?

After the family had eaten the children cleared the table.

A person reading this sentence might momentarily think that *the children* is the object of the verb *eaten*:

After the family had eaten the children

The reader might have to stop and mentally regroup the words to represent the correct meaning. Placing a comma at the end of the first clause prevents such confusion.

After the family had eaten, the children cleared the table.

However, when Pattern II is used, the conjunction separates the clauses, so a comma is not required.

The children cleared the table *after* the family had eaten.

Students are then shown how to use various subordinating conjunctions to create complex sentences. Here are some of the explanations and exercises for the conjunction *if.*

The conjunction *if* is called a "conditional" subordinating conjunction because it introduces the "condition" under which an event can occur. The following exercise asks you to write a complex sentence with a dependent clause expressing such a condition.

Exercise

Write a complex sentence with *if* used to create a dependent clause from the first sentence. Place the dependent clause in front of the independent clause.

> The snow keeps falling.
> Schools and government offices will be closed tomorrow.

Here is the answer for the last exercise.

> *If* the snow keeps falling, schools and government offices will be closed tomorrow.

The first clause presents the condition under which the action described in the second clause will occur.

Sometimes you can precede an independent clause with two dependent clauses. This pattern is shown in the following exercise.

Exercise

Transform the first two sentences into two dependent clauses by preceding each with *if.* Then write a sentence that begins with the two dependent clauses (connected with *and*) and ends with the third sentence.

> It doesn't rain soon.
> The days continue to be so hot.
> Our wheat crop will be ruined.

An engaging sentence can be created by preceding the main clause with three dependent clauses that progressively increase a reader's interest in the topic, as illustrated by the next exercise.

Exercise

Transform the first three sentences into three dependent clauses by preceding each with *if.* Then write a sentence that begins with the three dependent clauses (separated only by commas) and ends with the fourth sentence.

> Your story is developing well.
> The action and dialogue are moving towards the emotional core of your main characters.

The stakes for winning or losing have been raised higher and higher.

Your readers will experience increasing excitement as the conflict reaches its peak.

According to an *English Journal* article entitled "What High School Teachers Have to Say about Student Writing and Language Across the Curriculum," many students experience fear and apprehension when their reading assignments involve sentences containing subordinate clauses, especially sentences expressing cause-effect relationships with conjunctions such as *if, because, when,* and *since.* These students have a great deal of difficulty understanding textbooks in the fields of history and science, since cause-effect relationships are at the heart of knowledge in these fields. Teachers also report that students have trouble understanding "multiple-choice questions with subordinate clauses." The articles says, "students have difficulty determining the main idea of the sentence and thus the question; the subordinate clause leads to...confusion."

The author of the article, Trevor Gambell, suggests one way to deal with this difficulty: "This problem warns us that multiple choice questions need to be worded as simple sentences so that content is being tested rather than language." But Professor Ed Vavra, author of *Teaching Grammar as a Liberating Art*, is appalled by Gambell's suggestion and responds: "We should not, in other words, teach students how to understand complex sentences; rather, we should go down to their level. It is no wonder that college freshmen have trouble reading college-level texts."

A number of studies (reviewed in *Why Johnny Can't Write: How to Improve Writing Skills* by Linden and Whimbey) have found that students who constructed sentences in exercises like those shown in this book improved significantly on standardized tests of reading skills. Weak readers can understand short, simple sentences but have difficulty comprehending longer, complicated sentences containing more information and relationships. Apparently having them construct complicated sentences from simple ones prepares them to separate a complicated sentence into manageable chunks of information, interpret the chunks, and mentally reconstruct the full meaning of the sentence.

In fact, exercises on subordinating conjunctions have been specifically designed to encourage the careful mental processing that underlies strong reading skills. Here are two such exercises from a book entitled *Mastering Reading Through Reasoning* by Arthur Whimbey.

Exercises

Each exercise presents two conjunctions and two sentences. Read the sentences carefully and decide which conjunction could be placed before the first sentence to express the logical relationship between the two sentences. Then write the combined sentence with the conjunction placed before the first sentence and the resulting dependent clause placed before the second sentence.

1. combine these sentences using *if* or *when*.

   Jasmine stepped on her brake pedal.
   She realized that her driveway was a sheet of ice and that her car would not stop before reaching the closed garage door.

2. Combine these sentences using *before* or *if*.

   The United States helped the Cuban government institute a sanitation program In 1902.
   Cuba had been ravaged by yellow fever for years.

If you tried these two exercises, you probably noticed that the sentences must be read carefully in order to decide the appropriate conjunctions. Some teachers who use these exercises ask students to engage in an activity called DEAR (an acronym for *D*iscuss and *E*xplain *A*nswers and *R*easoning), which has proven particularly powerful for strengthening reading and reasoning skills. Students work separately in doing the exercises. Then each student compares his or her answer with those of another student. Wherever their answers differ, students explain to each other how they interpreted the sentences and what their reasoning was in choosing a conjunction. This activity provides students with quick feedback on the accuracy of their reading comprehension and reasoning. It also provides an incentive for reading and thinking carefully because the answers must be justified to another student. Students at Kent Johnson's Morningside Academy in Seattle gain more than two grade levels in reading skills per semester using *Mastering Reading Through Reasoning* and DEAR. Other educators have obtained similar gains at other schools. A book entitled *Thinkback* by Jack Lochhead describes how a similar method called TAPPS (Thinking Aloud Pair Problem Solving) has been used to improve reading and reasoning skills in several academic areas. Using sentence construction exercises to improve reading comprehension along with writing skills is discussed further in the next chapter, on relative clauses.

CHAPTER

12

RELATIVE CLAUSES

A relative clause is a grammatical structure that can be used to modify a noun with much more information than could be provided by just an adjective. Here is a sentence with an underlined relative clause.

Companies <u>which pollute the air or water</u> should be fined heavily.

Unfortunately, a significant number of students graduate from high school and enter college without having mastered the ability to express their ideas with relative clauses or comprehend relative clauses in the sentences of their textbooks. We will look at this problem in detail shortly, after we illustrate how the P-C Approach teaches students the various characteristics of relative clauses:

The underlined group of words in the following sentence is called a relative clause. It provides more information about the noun *animals*.

> Animals <u>which are in danger of extinction</u> must not be captured or injured.

Here are two sentences that together express the same information as the above sentence.

1. Some animals must not be captured or injured.
2. The animals are in danger of extinction.

You can see that Sentence 2 provides the same information about the noun *animals* that the relative clause does in the above sentence. The two sentences are combined into the above sentence by using the following steps.

> Step 1. The noun *animals* (along with *the*) in sentence 2 is replaced by *which*.
>
> > *The animals* are in danger of extinction.
> > *which* are in danger of extinction

> Step 2. This relative clause is inserted into Sentence 1 right after *animals* because it provides more information about *animals*.
>
> > Animals *which are in danger of extinction* must not be captured or injured.

Note that in combining the sentences, *some* is deleted from Sentence 1 because the specific animals are identified by the relative clause.

Note also that we let *which* stand for the noun *animals* in Sentence 2. Since *which* stands for a noun, it is a pronoun. But it is given a special name. It is called a RELATIVE PRONOUN.

As far as we know, calling *which* a "relative" pronoun makes no more nor less sense than calling a rock a "rock." It is just the name given to this type of pronoun. Some grammar books say that it is called "relative" because it is *related* to the noun it modifies. But all pronouns are related to their antecedents, so this explanation is not very convincing.

Sample Exercise

Rewrite the first sentence with the information from the second added as a relative clause.

> The car was being driven by a drunk person whose license had been suspended for DWI.
> The car killed my wife and son.

Answer Explanation

The second sentence provides more information about the car. Therefore, *the car* is replaced by *which* to form a relative clause.

> *The car* killed my wife and son.
> *which* killed my wife and son

This relative clause is inserted after *car* in the first sentence.

> The car *which killed my wife and son* was being driven by a drunk person whose license had been suspended for DWI.

Next, students are shown the difference between essential and nonessential relative clauses, along with the punctuation appropriate for each. Here is the explanation we present in *Keys to Quick Writing Skills* by Whimbey, Williams, and Linden.

Both of the following sentences contain WHICH, but only the first has commas.

> Automobiles, *which were invented around 1900*, should be cheaper.
>   ↑   ↑
>   comma   comma

> Automobiles *which produce excessive smoke* should be illegal.

Why does the first sentence have commas but the second does not? Try dropping "which were invented around 1900" from the first sentence:

> Automobiles should be cheaper.

This sentence still has basically the same meaning. The part dropped is not *essential* information. It is extra information, so it is set off by commas.

However, try dropping "which produce excessive smoke" from the second sentence:

> Automobiles should be illegal.

This sentence now has a drastically different meaning from the original sentence. It no longer bans just rolling smog factories but all cars. Most people would support the original sentence but fight the shortened version, loving their automobiles as life itself. The information dropped is essential not extra, so it is not set off by commas.

> Essential Information—No Commas
> Nonessential Information—Set Off By Commas

Sample Exercise

Rewrite the first sentence with the information from the second added as a relative clause set off by commas.

> William Shakespeare's plays are still widely enjoyed in England where people share their historical background and symbols.

> The plays were written in London around 1600.

Answer Explanation

The second sentence provides more information about the plays. *The plays* is replaced by *which* to form a relative clause.

> *The plays* were written in London around 1600.
> *which* were written in London around 1600

This relative clause modifies *plays*, so it is inserted after *plays* in the first sentence.

> William Shakespeare's plays, which were written in London around 1600, are still widely enjoyed in England where people share their historical background and symbols.

Exercises

Rewrite the first sentence with the information from the second added as a relative clause set off by commas.

> The Globe Playhouse saw its final curtain fall in 1644 when it was torn down by mercenary land developers to build houses.

> The Globe Playhouse was the home of Shakespeare's acting company.

The lesson on essential and nonessential relative clauses illustrates the importance of understanding grammatical concepts in punctuating a sentence properly. Many students rain commas somewhat haphazardly upon a sentence. Others seem to employ a policy of inserting a comma after a fair number of words have been written. Their rule for comma usage is that long stretches of words require periodic commas. Trying to teach students to use commas correctly will remain a frustrating task until they understand the grammatical structures related to comma usage, including nonessential relative clauses, dependent clauses placed before independent clauses, coordinated clauses (in contrast to coordinated phrases), prepositional phrases, and others discussed in later chapters.

Here is how some of the other aspects of relative clauses are taught to students.

A relative clause can modify a noun occurring anywhere in a sentence. Here is a sentence with the relative clause at the end.

> Next year my company is moving to Phoenix, *which* is a little too hot in the summer but very pleasant in the winter.

Note that the relative clause is set off with a comma because the information it presents is not essential in identifying the city. Note also that only one comma is needed when a nonessential relative clause is placed at the end of a sentence.

In the next sentence, the relative clause is not set off with a comma. The writer considers this relative clause essential because it identifies the storm as very severe.

> According to the weather report, we should prepare for a storm *which* could paralyze the city.

Exercises

1. Rewrite the first sentence with the information from the second added as a relative clause set off by a comma.

   Twelve-year-old Kathy Watson started a business called Kathy's Creations.

   Kathy's Creations sold $5,000 worth of hand-painted Christmas ornaments last year.

2. Rewrite the first sentence with the information from the second added as a relative clause. A comma is not needed.

   Many college students are majoring in fields related to computers to prepare for professions.

   The professions should be viable and well-paying for as long as they live.

So far you have created relative clauses by replacing the subjects of sentences with *which*. However, a relative clause can often be created by substituting *which* for a noun in another position of a sentence. Compare these sentences.

> The *files* included the birth records of many older citizens,
>
> The fire destroyed the *files*.

Note that the noun *files* appears in both sentences. To add the information from the second sentence to the first, replace *the files* with *which*.

> The fire destroyed *the files*.
>
> The fire destroyed *which*

Move *which* to the front to create a relative clause.

which the fire destroyed

Insert this relative clause into the first sentence right after the noun that *which* represents: *files*.

relative clause

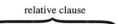

The *files* which the fire destroyed included the birth records of many older citizens.

The relative clause is not set off by commas because it is essential in identifying the files that included the records.

Exercises

1. Transform the second sentence into a relative clause by replacing the underlined words with *which*. Move *which* to the front to form a relative clause. Then rewrite the first sentence with this relative clause added right after the noun it modifies.

   An unknown writer will be most successful if he can offer a magazine editor an article.

   The permanent staff of the magazine could not write <u>the article</u> because of its specialized content or unique style.

2. Rewrite the first sentence with the information from the second added as a relative clause.

   The motorcycle costs more than my car.

   My son wants the motorcycle as a graduation present.

The word *that* can be used as a relative pronoun. However, it can only be used in essential relative clauses, not in nonessential relative clauses. Here are the answers for the last two exercises with *that* used instead of *which*.

   An unknown writer will be most successful if he can offer a magazine editor an article *that* the permanent staff of the magazine could not write because of its specialized content or unique style.

   The motorcycle *that* my son wants as a graduation present costs more than my car.

Exercise

Rewrite the first sentence with the information from the second added as a relative clause with the relative pronoun *that*.

> Mr. Jones asked to see the maintenance record for the airplane.
>
> His son wants to buy the airplane.

The relative pronouns *which* and *that* are used in referring to inanimate objects and animals. However, *who* is the relative pronoun used in referring to humans. In the following sentence, the underlined relative clause begins with *who*.

> Alexander Graham Bell, who invented the telephone, had a deaf wife.

The procedure for constructing sentences with relative clauses using *who* is similar to the procedure for *which*: Replace a noun in one sentence with *who* and move *who* to the front if it is not already there. Then add the resulting relative clause to the other sentence right after the noun it modifies.

Exercises

1. Rewrite the first sentence with the information from the second added as a relative clause set off with commas.

    Thomas Edison asserted that creativity is 10 percent inspiration and 90 percent perspiration.

    Thomas Edison invented electric lights and movies.

2. Rewrite the first sentence with the information from the second added as a relative clause. Commas are not needed.

    A hiker was chased away by the frightening mother bear when she returned from wherever she had been.

    The hiker unintentionally came upon some grizzly bear cubs.

A relative pronoun can be omitted from an essential relative clause if the relative pronoun replaces an object (rather than a subject). For example, here is the answer from a previous exercise.

> The motorcycle *which* my son wants as a graduation present costs more than my car.

Which can be deleted from the sentence.

> The motorcycle my son wants as a graduation present costs more than my car.

Here is another sentence that we analyzed earlier.

Animals *which* are in danger of extinction must not be captured or injured.

Notice that deleting *which* produces a faulty sentence.

Wrong: Animals are in danger of extinction must not be captured or injured.

The problem with this sentence is that *animals* is followed by two complete predicates.

Animals are in danger of extinction must not be captured or injured.

predicate   predicate

The reason for the problem is that *which* represents the subject in the relative clause.

The animals are in danger of extinction.

which are in danger of extinction

subject position

But in the sentence about the motorcycle, *which* represents the object in the relative clause.

My son wants *the motorcycle* as a graduation present.

My son wants *which*   as a graduation present

object position

When deleting a relative pronoun is grammatically permissible, you have a choice on whether or not to do so. Sometimes deleting a relative pronoun makes a sentence crisper. Other times it makes the sentence sound awkward or too informal for its purpose (as with a job application letter). When you proofread something you have written, if you see a relative pronoun that can be omitted, try omitting it and then decide whether or not its omission improves the sentence.

Incidentally, did you notice that a relative pronoun was omitted from the first dependent clause in the last sentence? Here is the dependent clause with the omitted relative pronoun in parenthesis:

When you proofread something (that) you have written

If you did not notice that the relative pronoun was omitted when you first read the sentence, then we were correct in omitting it. An omitted relative pronoun should not make a sentence sound awkward or unusual (as if something is missing) to a reader who is concentrating on meaning.

Exercise

Rewrite the first sentence with the information from the second added as a relative clause with the relative pronoun omitted.

> The short story is very exciting.
> Kendra wrote the short story for her English class.

Bill's is the possessive form of the noun *Bill*. The possessive form of the relative pronouns *which*, *that*, and *who* is *whose*. Here is a sentence with *whose* underlined.

> The woman <u>whose</u> jewelry store was totally destroyed by the flames requested a thorough investigation into the cause of the fire.

This sentence can be analyzed into the following two sentences.

> The woman requested a thorough investigation into the cause of the fire.
> The woman's jewelry store was totally destroyed by the flames.

To combine the sentences, first *the woman's* is replaced by *whose*.

> *The woman's* jewelry store was totally destroyed by the flames.
> *whose* jewelry store was totally destroyed by the flames

Then this relative clause is inserted into the first sentence after the noun (*woman*) it refers to.

relative clause

The woman *whose* jewelry store was totally destroyed by the flames requested a thorough investigation into the cause of the fire.

Exercise

Rewrite the first sentence with the information from the second added as a relative clause.

> A young lady asked us for a ride home.
> The lady's bicycle had a flat tire.

In the last exercise the possessive noun (*lady's*) is at the beginning of the sentence, so when it was replaced by *whose*, *whose* did not have to be moved to the beginning in order to form a reflective clause. But consider this sentence.

Pete found the man's dog.

When *the man's* is replaced by *whose*, and *whose* is moved to the front, *dog* comes along with *whose*.

Pete found *whose* dog

whose dog Pete found

Dog travels along to the front with the possessive pronoun (*whose*) so that the reader sees what is possessed (*dog*).

The resulting relative clause could be added to this sentence.

The man sent two basketball tickets to Pete.

The man *whose dog Pete found* sent two basketball tickets to Pete.

relative clause

Exercises

Rewrite the first sentence with the information from the second added as a relative clause.

The gym instructor designs excellent routines for new club members.

I borrowed the instructor's workout gloves.

Let us now examine the problem mentioned at the beginning of this chapter: the difficulty that some students have comprehending textbooks containing sentences with relative clauses. Here is a paragraph from the *Encyclopedia Americana*.

> **Infectious diseases are the only ones that can be transmitted. They may be spread by infected animals, infected people, or contaminated substances, such as food and water. Infectious diseases that can be transmitted to humans from infected animals are known as zoonoses. Zoonoses may be transmitted by carriers, such as insects; by the bite of an infected animal; by direct contact with an infected animals or its excretions; or by eating animal products.**

College freshman were asked to read this paragraph and then answer the following question.

Zoonoses are:

a. insects that carry diseases.

b. infected animals that transmit infectious diseases to humans.

c. infectious diseases that man gets from animals.

d. carriers that transmit infectious diseases.

College students with weak reading skills often pick alternative b. When asked why they picked b, some reply that *zoonoses* sounds like *zoo*, and animals are kept in zoos, so they figured zoonoses are animals. This explanation reflects the thinking style of nonanalytical readers. They base their conclusions on superficial associations among bits of information rather than on careful step-by-step interpretations of chunks of information and gradual reconstruction of total meaning.

Other students who chose b explained that they got this answer from the last six words of the third sentence: infected animals are known as zoonoses. This, too, reflects the thinking style of weak readers. They read a little bit here, a little bit there, and then jump to a conclusion.

The correct answer is based on the third sentence, which reads:

Infectious diseases that can be transmitted to humans from infected animals are known as zoonoses.

This sentence contains the following relative clause.

that can be transmitted to humans from infected animals

Good readers work step-by-step through the sentence in obtaining its correct meaning. They begin with the subject: infectious diseases. Then they go on to the relative clause, an essential relative clause that indicates the type of infectious diseases being considered: those that animals can transmit to humans. Finally, they come to the predicate: are known as zoonoses. Therefore, in answering the question they pick alternative c.

Research studies have found that students with weak analytical skills can understand only simple sentences, just as they can solve only one-step math problems. They have difficulty understanding complicated sentences, just as they have difficulty solving multi-step math problems. In other words, they can handle just small chucks of information because they have not developed skill in working step-by-step through complicated information. They can understand sentences such as this:

Some infectious diseases are known as zoonoses.

But they cannot understand Sentence 3 in the paragraph.

Other research studies (reviewed in *Why Johnny can't Write: How to Improve Writing Skills*) have found that having students construct complex sentences from simple ones improves their scores on standardized reading tests. These studies have not explored whether having students add relative clauses to sentences improves their ability to comprehend specifically sentences with relative clauses. They have only found that constructing various types of complicated sentences from simpler ones (using the types of exercises shown in this book) improves overall reading comprehension ability, with the weakest readers making the greatest gains. As the P-C Approach is used more widely in our schools, we can expect the average reading comprehension ability of the nation to improve. And as this improvement becomes evident, researchers may conduct additional studies to determine exactly how and why having students manipulate, construct, and write sentences improves their reading skills.

CHAPTER
13

MODALS FOR EXTENDING THE MEANINGS OF VERBS

Modals are helping verbs that are used to express capability, intention, obligation, permission, insistence, possibility, and other such ideas about actions and events. Modals are not very complicated, so they are easy to teach. Nevertheless, many traditional grammar texts neglect them, leaving an entire area of grammar to remain a mystery to students. Worse yet, many of the texts that do not teach modals exacerbate students' confusion and lack of confidence by requiring them to identify modals as part of the verb phrases in sentences. Our P-C workbook devotes an entire chapter to modals, with this beginning:

> Modals are helping verbs—words that are used with verbs to change their meanings somewhat and thus expand the number of ideas that can

be expressed with verbs. For example, here is a simple sentence with the verb *sell*.

Jim *sells* magazine subscriptions.

Now here is the sentence with the modal *might* before the verb.

Jim *might* sell magazine subscriptions.

Adding *might* changes the meaning of the sentence from telling what Jim does to telling what he may do some time in the future.

Some students find the term *modals* strange and unfamiliar. However, modals are easy to use yet very useful. Just remember that modals are simple helping verbs, which means that they are used with main verbs to extend the meanings of the verbs. There are only eight modals. In addition to *might*, the other modals are *can, could, will, would, should, must*, and *may*.

Note that one of the modals listed in the last sentence is *will*. This modal was already discussed in Chapters 3 and 4. It is used to make statements about the future. The following sentences illustrate the difference between *will* and *might*.

Detroit *will* build two new libraries.

Detroit *might* build two new libraries.

Both sentences make statements about the future. However, the sentence with *will* says the libraries are definitely going to be built, whereas the sentence with *might* is less definite: It says that there is a chance they are going to be built.

Exercises

1. Rewrite this sentence with *might* replaced by *should*.

   Tulane might give Harold Garcia a basketball scholarship.

2. Rewrite this sentence with *can* replaced by *must*.

   Jennifer can take the chemistry exam on Friday.

The above exercises illustrate meanings for four modals: *might, should. can*, and *must*.

Let us look at two grammatical characteristics of modals. To begin, consider this sentence.

Mr. Chavez *teaches* geology.

Notice that the verb in the above sentence is *teaches*. This is the form of the verb *teach* appropriate for the singular subject *Mr. Chavez*. But notice what happens to the verb when *can* is inserted before it.

Mr. Chavez *can teach* geology.

The main verb now has its base form *teach*. When a modal is inserted before a verb, the verb always takes its base form.

The second interesting characteristic of modals is that they do not change form. Compare these sentences.

Joe can teach swimming.
Frank and Martha can teach swimming.

Whether the subject is singular (*Joe*) or plural (*Frank and Martha*), the modal (*can*) has the same form.

Exercises

In each sentence, the underlined verb is not quite correct for expressing the idea that the writer wants to communicate. Rewrite the sentence with the modal in parenthesis inserted before the underlined verb.

1. (can) Mom <u>drives</u> us to school after she gets her license.
2. (must) Jack <u>exercises</u> regularly if he plans to stay in shape.

All the modals have more than one meaning. This does not lead to confusion because the appropriate meaning of a modal in a particular sentence is generally obvious from the context. For example, *may* can be used to mean that an action is likely to occur, as in this sentence.

I *may* go to the library tonight, but I'm not sure.

However, *may* is also used in expressing permission, as in the next sentence.

You *may* borrow my book, but don't write in it.

To take another example, the modal *can* is used to express capability:

Mark *can* do squats with 300 pounds on his back.

The modal *can* is also used to express permission:

You *can* use my room while I am at camp.

Furthermore, the modal *can* is used in making polite requests:

Can you please hold this package for me?

This sentence is not asking a person whether he or she is capable of holding the package. It is politely asking for a favor.

Some old grammar books insisted that *can* should not be used to indicate permission: only *may* should be used for permission. However, *can* has a long history of usage by respected writers for indicating both ability and permission. Therefore, modern linguists do not oppose the use of *can* for granting permission. In fact, while *can* or *may* could be used in the underlined position of the next sentence, *can* sounds more idiomatic.

> Since I won't be needing the car tonight, the boys can/may use it to go to the basketball game.

The following exercises illustrate two meanings for the modal *must*.

Exercises

Rewrite each sentence with the underlined words and commas replaced by *must*.

1. Martin is required to work overtime tonight to repair a gas leak in a pipe.
2. Phil does, I am led to conclude, drink a lot of soda because his garbage can is always full of soda bottles.

The chapter on modals in the P-C workbook not only explains the use of modals. It also gives students additional practice in recognizing verbs in sentences and draws their attention to various words that can be used as verbs. These experiences add to students' ability to identify the verbs in any sentences.

Chapter 2 shows eight sentences of the type that many traditional grammar texts present to students with the instructions to underline the verb in each. This task is generally imposed on students before they have had any instruction on modals but with just the definition that "a verb expresses an action or state of being," followed by a few sample sentences containing a variety of advanced verb phrases. Here is one of the sentences from Chapter 2.

> Before entering the Jacuzzi, you must take a shower.

If students underline *entering* or *take*, they are told that their answer is incorrect, that the verb is *must take*. This experience not only discourages students from believing that they can learn grammar. It also contributes to the negative attitude that many at-risk students develop towards education and that eventually leads to their becoming dropouts condemned to minimum-wage jobs.

The P-C Approach does not demand that students know that modals can be part of a verb phrase until it teaches students about modals. In fact, it never asks students to identify modals in sentences because this task has never proven to have any value. Instead, it asks students to add modals to sentences in order to express various types of meaning. It thus reinforces and expands the repertoire of grammatical structures that students have for expressing their ideas in writing.

Incidentally, students learn why *entering* is not the verb in the above sentence about the Jacuzzi when they study gerunds, an advanced structure that is discussed later in this book.

CHAPTER
14

USING **HAVE** AS A MAIN VERB AND AS A HELPING VERB IN FORMING THE PERFECT TENSES

A traditional handbook on writing skills by an English professor tells students on the second page of the verb chapter that main verbs have three principal parts: a simple form, a past tense, and a past participle. The simple form, says this professor, shows present tense action, occurrence, or state of being. It is also used with *will* to form the future tense. The past tense indicates action, occurrence, or state of being completed in the past. The past tense of regular verbs adds *d* or *ed* to the simple form. But there are many irregular verbs that form the past tense in different ways. The past participle of regular verbs has the same form as the past tense, but for irregular verbs the past participle is generally different. Students should memorize the principal parts of irregular verbs, advises this professor, to make writing easier. A past participle functions as a verb only when it is combined with an auxiliary verb, as in the sentence *They were startled*, with *were* being the auxiliary verb, *startled* the past participle, and *were startled* the verb phrase. A past participle used alone functions as an adjective, modifying nouns and pronouns.

All of the above terms and concepts are presented on the second page, when most students hardly understand what a verb is. The professor recognizes that some students might find this presentation confusing. In the instructor's edition she tells teachers: "Some students may be overwhelmed by verb tenses." What is her solution to the problem? The traditional one: more terminology and complexity. She suggests: "It may be helpful to show them the basic distinction between tense and aspect." ". . . *Aspect* says something about the way the action is experienced. The progressive aspect (*to be* + *ing*) shows an action still in progress and the perfect aspect (*has, have,* or *had* + past participle) shows a completed action or one being continued into the present from a specific point in the past."

This text does not provide what Robert DeBeaugrande, who is quoted in Chapter 2, calls the "lower rungs" of the grammar ladder. It ensures that many students never understand higher-level grammatical concepts because students are not given a solid footing for taking the first steps in understanding the fundamental concepts.

The P-C Approach introduces students to the present, past, and future verb tenses systematically over the course of one entire chapter. The auxiliary verb *were* mentioned above is introduced in another chapter devoted to the special verb *be* (*were* is a form of *be*). The progressive tense is likewise introduced in the *be* chapter because progressive verb phrases always involve a form of *be*. The past participle and the perfect tenses are advanced concepts that warrant yet another complete chapter if students are expected to understand them. Furthermore, the P-C Approach presents these concepts in the context of constructing meaningful sentences. Here is how the chapter on the perfect tenses begins:

> The word *have* and its variations (*has, had*) are among the most frequently used words in English. This is true partly because *have* is really two words: a main verb and a helping verb. First we will discuss the use of *have* as a main verb. Then we will turn to its central role in creating what are called the "perfect" tenses, which allow a writer to describe time relationships more fully and accurately.
>
> *Have* can be used as a main verb to mean "possess, include, or contain"

as in this sentence.

> Some houses *have* termites.

In the above sentence, the subject (*houses*) is plural, so the plural form of the verb (*have*) is used. Notice how the verb *have* changes when the subject is singular.

> Our house *has* termites.

Have is an irregular verb because its singular form is not written by just adding *s* to the base form. Instead, the singular form is *has*.

Exercises

Rewrite each sentence with *have* or *has* in the blank space.

1. My girlfriend_____a tattoo.

2. Mangos _____ a rich delicious flavor.

You know from the earlier chapters on verbs that when the subject of a sentence is *you* or *I*, the appropriate present tense verb is not the one used with other singular subjects. In the case of the verb *have*, when the subject of a sentence is *you* or *I*, the correct present tense form is the base form (*have*) not the *s* form (*has*). This table shows the correct form of *have* for singular subjects except *you* or *I*, and for plural subjects as well as *you* or *I*.

Present Tense Forms of HAVE

Singular Subjects Except You or I	Plural Subjects And You or I
has	have

Exercises

Each sentence is composed of two clauses with the verb omitted from each. Rewrite each sentence with *have* in one blank and *has* in the other.

1. My roommate Loretta _____ three fish, and I _____a turtle.
2. You _____ some extra money for investment, and Daryl _____ the computer skills needed to run an e-mail business.

The past tense form of *have* is *had*, as illustrated by this sentence.

> I *had* a raccoon for a pet when I was young.

Exercise

Rewrite this sentence with the past tense form of *have*.

> Yolanda has a cabin near Lake Tahoe.

In addition to being used as a main verb, *have* is also an important "helping verb." It is used with a main verb to change the time or "tense" represented by the main verb. Compare these sentences:

> Gwen left when Tom got home.
> Gwen had left when Tom got home.

Sentence 1 says that when Tom got home, Gwen then left. Perhaps she waited until Tom got home because she was caring for their children.

However, Sentence 2 says that by the time Tom got home, Gwen had already left. The word *had* puts one event (*left*) before the other event (*got home*).

Sentences 1 and 2 illustrate that *had* can be used as a helping verb to show clearly that one event in the past occurred before another event in the past. In this usage *had* is called a helping verb because it is used in conjunction with the main verb *left*.

When *have* is used as a helping verb, it does not have the same meaning as it does as a main verb. Many words have different meanings in different contexts. Compare these sentences.

> 1. Leo got a letter.
> 2. Leo got lost.

In Sentence 1, "got" means "received." But *got* does not mean "received" in Sentence 2. We would not say, *Leo received lost*. Similarly, when *have* is used as a helping verb it does not mean "possess" or "contain." It simply changes the time (tense) expressed by the main verb.

Let us examine the above sentences further.

> Gwen *left* when Tom got home.
> Gwen *had left* when Tom got home.

Left is the past tense form of the verb *leave*. When *had* is placed before *left*, the resulting verb phrase (*had left*) is called the "past perfect tense."

The term "past perfect" is derived from the fact that the word *perfect* can mean roughly "complete." Something that is completed is perfected.

The past perfect tense indicates that one event had been "completed" before another event occurred. Gwen's leaving had been completed before Tom arrived.

To form the past perfect tense in the example above, *had* was inserted before *left*.

Gwen *had* left before Tom got home.

Exercise

Rewrite this sentence with *had* inserted before *remembered*.

If Paul remembered to bring his textbook to the dentist's office, he could have read his homework assignment while waiting for the dentist.

Here is the answer to the above exercise.

If Paul *had* remembered to bring his textbook to the dentist's office, he could have read his homework assignment while waiting for the dentist.

Sometimes the form of a verb must be changed when *had* is inserted before it. Try this exercise.

Exercise

Rewrite this sentence with *had* inserted before the underlined verb. Change the form of the verb if necessary.

If Harry <u>drew</u> a map for us, we would not have gotten lost.

Here is the answer to the above exercise.

If Harry *had drawn* a map for us, we would not have gotten lost.

Note that when *had* is inserted into the sentence, the verb changes from *drew* to *drawn*. To understand why, let us begin by reviewing past tense forms of regular and irregular verbs.

Recall from the verb chapter that the past tense of a regular verb is constructed by adding *ed* to the base form.

Regular Verb

<u>Base Form</u>	<u>Past Tense</u>
work	worked

However, the past tense of irregular verbs takes various forms. For example, the past tense of *draw* is *drew*.

Irregular Verb

Base Form	Past Tense
draw	drew

For the past perfect tense, a verb form called the past participle is needed. For regular verbs, the past participle has the same form as the past tense.

Regular Verb

Base Form	Past Tense	Past Participle
work	worked	worked

But for irregular verbs, the past participle can take various forms. The past participle of *draw* is shown in this table.

Irregular Verb

Base Form	Past Tense	Past Participle
draw	drew	drawn

In the following exercise, you will need to use the past participle form of *see*, which is shown in this table.

Irregular Verb

Base Form	Past Tense	Past Participle
see	saw	seen

Exercise

Rewrite this sentence with *had* inserted before the appropriate form of *see* to emphasize the time relationship between the two events described in the sentence.

> I saw the movie three times already, so I did not enjoy watching it again last night.

For the next exercise you will need the past participle of the verb *be*.

Some forms of BE

Base Form	Past Tense	Past Participle
be	was/were	been

Exercise

Rewrite this sentence with *had* inserted before the appropriate form of *be* to emphasize the time relationship between the two events described in the sentence.

> Betty was overweight for years before she got married.

An earlier chapter explained that a verb phrase like *was trying* is called the past progressive tense because it concerns an action that was in progress or continued over a period of time in the past. This verb phrase can be transformed into the past perfect progressive tense by preceding it with *had* and changing *was* to *been*, as illustrated by the next exercise.

Exercise

Rewrite this sentence with *had* inserted before the appropriate form of *be*.

> Crystal was trying to call you for two hours before you called her.

If you are unsure about the form of the past participle for a verb, look the verb up in the dictionary. If the verb is a regular verb, the past participle will not be shown. This generally means that you just add *ed* or *d* to the base verb to form the past participle. But if the verb is an irregular verb, the past participle will generally be shown.

In addition to the past perfect tense, there is another perfect tense called the present perfect tense. To understand the purpose of the present perfect tense, compare these sentences and decide which person still lives in Chicago—Ruby or Gene?

1. Ruby *lived* in Chicago for three years.

2. Gene *has lived* in Chicago for three years.

Sentence 1 uses the past tense verb (*lived*), indicating that Ruby's residence in Chicago is a thing of the past. But sentence 2 suggests that Gene still lives there.

Sentence 2 uses the present perfect verb phrase *has lived*. A present perfect verb phrase is constructed by placing a present tense form of *have* in front of the past participle of the main verb.

> Present Perfect Tense = Have/Has + Past Participle

Note that *have* has two present tense forms—*have* and *has*. The one to use depends on the subject. If the subject is singular, *has* is required.

> Cristina *has* been in the army for two years.

But if the subject is plural, *have* is appropriate.

Charlie and Martha *have* loved each other since high school.

Let's spend a minute more looking at the meaning of the present perfect tense. Here is one of the above sentences rewritten with the simple past tense verb *was*:

Christina *was* in the army for two years.

The past tense verb *was* indicates that Cristina served in the army at some time in the past. It suggests that she is no longer in the army. But suppose she is still in the army. The present tense verb *is* cannot be used because the sentence contains the phrase *for two years*:

Wrong: Christina *is* in the army for two years.

Therefore, the present perfect tense must be used.

Cristina *has been* in the army for two years.

Thus, we see that the present perfect is used for an action, event, or situation that began in the past and continues into the present.

The present perfect also has another common interpretation. It can be used for an action, event, or situation that occurred in the past but is still relevant to the present. Consider this sentence.

The Red Cross *has offered* to send food and medical supplies to the flood victims.

The offer occurred in the past, but the sentence suggests that the offer is still in effect; the Red Cross is still willing to send the food and supplies if needed.

In summary, here are the forms for the simple past tense, past perfect, and present perfect for a regular verb.

	Simple Past	Past Perfect	Present Perfect
Regular Verb	worked	had worked	have/has worked

And here are the forms for the simple past tense, past perfect, and present perfect for an irregular verb.

	Simple Past	Past Perfect	Present Perfect
Irregular Verb	ate	had eaten	have/has eaten

Exercises

Rewrite each sentence with the underlined verb written in the present perfect tense.

1.   Luis and Yvonne <u>played</u> golf together for many years.

2.   The United States <u>was</u> a democracy since 1776.

A student who has gone through the above explanations and exercises (along with the additional exercises in the workbook) could rewrite the following sentence with *was* replaced by a past perfect verb to express the time relationship more fully.

> Mr. Robinson *was* the assistant coach for ten years before being promoted to head coach.

The student would write:

> Mr. Robinson *had been* the assistant coach for ten years before being promoted to head coach.

This sentence is included in chapter 2 to illustrate the types of sentences that traditional grammar texts often present to students (after just a brief explanation of verbs) with the instructions to underline the verbs. Many students are stumped by the task.

Students can learn to recognize and use the perfect tenses. But this learning cannot occur with the inadequate instruction found in most traditional grammar texts. The opening paragraphs of this chapter present an example of how a traditional text bombards students with the terms *past participle* and *perfect aspect (tense)*, along with *auxiliary verb, irregular verb,* and *progressive aspect* all at the very beginning of its verb chapter. Such texts torture students on the rack of mental confusion and frustration year after year, scarring them with a lifelong fear or hatred of grammar. By contrast, the gradual but thorough lessons of the P-C Approach give students an appreciation of how a knowledge of grammar can make writing more satisfying and enjoyable.

CHAPTER
15

VOICE: ACTIVE AND PASSIVE

Merriam-Webster's definition of a verb quoted in chapter 2 says that a verb can be inflected for voice. This characteristic of verbs refers to the fact that a sentence may be written in the active or passive voice. The verb of a passive sentence has a distinct form, and students should learn to recognize that form so they can avoid passive sentences that are unnecessarily wordy or weak. Because active sentences are simpler and more common than their passive counterparts, the P-C Approach begins with active sentences and shows students how to transform them into passive sentences. When students make these transformations themselves, their attention is drawn to all the details that distinguish active from passive sentences. Next students are shown how to make the opposite transformation: from passive to active. Writing teachers have found that some inexperienced writers overload their papers and reports with passive sentences when active sentences could make the same points more strongly and succinctly. Having students practice transforming sentences from passive to active helps them avoid this problem. The chapter on voice in the P-C workbook begins with the prototype sentence that has proven so useful for introducing students to verbs and other fundamental concepts:

Here is a sentence with an action verb.

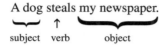

The subject (*A dog*) performs the action, and the object (*my newspaper*) receives the action. Compare the above sentence to the next one.

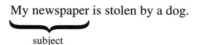

In this sentence, the subject (*my newspaper*) is the thing that receives the action, and *a dog* is at the end of the sentence.

The first sentence below is called an active sentence, and the second is called a passive sentence.

Active: A dog steals my newspaper.

Passive: My newspaper is stolen by a dog.

The first sentence is called active because the subject performs the action. The word "passive" means "not active" or "acted on by some outside force." The second sentence is called passive because the subject does not perform the action. It receives the action.

Let us examine the parts of a passive sentence more fully.

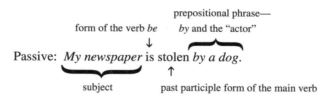

A passive sentence contains the following parts:

1. A subject that receives the action.
2. A form of the verb *be*.
3. The past participle form of the main verb.
4. A prepositional phrase consisting of the preposition *by* and the person or thing that performs the action.

Here are the steps for transforming an active sentence with a present tense verb into a passive sentence.

Step 1. Make the object of the active sentence the subject of the passive sentence.

Step 2. Add *is* or *are* after the new subject. Add *is* if the new subject is singular and *are* if it is plural.

Step 3. Change the main verb to its past participle form.

Step 4. Place the subject of the active sentence at the end, preceded by the preposition *by*.

Use these steps in this sample exercise.

Sample Exercise

Transform this sentence into a passive sentence.

Cigarettes cause cancer.

Answer Explanation

Step 1. The object of the active sentence is *cancer*. It becomes the subject of the passive sentence.

Cancer

Step 2. Since the new subject is singular, *is* is added.

Cancer is

Step 3. The past participle form of *cause* is *caused.*

Cancer is caused

Step 4. The subject of the active sentence (*cigarettes*) is placed at the end, preceded by the word *by*.

Cancer is caused by cigarettes.

In the last exercise, the verb is regular. Therefore, the past participle is formed by just adding *d*. In the next exercise, the verb is irregular. Also, in the last exercise, the new subject (*cancer*) is singular, so *is* follows the subject. In the next exercise, the new subject is plural. Try this sample exercise before reading the answer. Refer to the steps listed above and to the last sample exercise if needed for guidance.

Sample Exercise

Rewrite this sentence as a passive sentence.

> Insects eat my strawberries.

Answer Explanation

Step 1. The object of the active sentence is *my strawberries*. It becomes the subject of the passive sentence.

> My strawberries

Step 2. Since the new subject is plural, *are* is added.

> My strawberries are

Step 3. The past participle form of *eat* is *eaten*.

> My strawberries are eaten

Step 4. The subject of the active sentence (*insects*) is placed at the end, preceded by the word *by*.

> My strawberries are eaten by insects.

Exercise

Rewrite this sentence as a passive sentence.

> 1. Children watch cartoons.

Notice that the past participle is used in writing passive sentences. This is the same verb form used in writing perfect tense sentences.

However, there is no connection between the two types of sentences. Just as many words have two meanings, the past participle has two uses: It is used for the perfect tenses and for the passive voice. Furthermore, it is called the past participle because when it is used in sentences with perfect tenses, it refers to events that occurred in the past. However, when it is used in passive sentences, it does not necessarily refer to past events. The two sample exercises you just completed both involve the present tense.

The active sentences we have so far transformed to passive form have present tense verbs, so the form of *be* in the passive sentences has been the present tense forms *is* or *are*. But when an active sentence with a past tense verb is made passive, the form of *be* is one of the past tense forms *was* or *were*. Whether *was* or *were* is used depends, of course, on whether the new subject is singular or plural.

Here are the four steps for forming a passive sentence from an active sentence with a past tense verb.

Step 1. Make the object of the active sentence the subject of the passive sentence.

Step 2. Add *was* or *were* after the new subject. Add *was* if the new subject is singular and *were* if it is plural.

Step 3. Change the main verb to its past participle form.

Step 4. Place the subject of the active sentence at the end, preceded by the preposition *by*.

Exercise

Rewrite this sentence in passive form.

Everyone enjoyed the party.

Active sentences tend to be more powerful than passive sentences. One reason is that active sentences are generally less wordy than passive sentences. Compare these sentences.

Active: My dog drank my chocolate shake.

Passive: My chocolate shake was drunk by my dog.

form of *be*   preposition *by*

Note that the active sentence has only six words, whereas the passive sentence has eight words. The two extra words in the passive sentence are the verb *be* and the preposition *by*. Thus, active sentences are often more efficient: They say the same thing with fewer words.

Furthermore, active sentences tend to be more dynamic—they pack more punch—because the person or thing performing the action is the subject. Active sentences do not push the active agent to the back of the sentence. Also, the verbs in active sentences tend to be more vivid. The verb phrases in passive sentences always start with forms of *be*, which are duller than action verbs.

Inexperienced writers sometimes write passive sentences unconsciously or unintentionally. They do not realize that they could express the same idea more effectively with an active sentence. When you proofread anything that you have written, be on the lookout for passive sentences. See whether you could express the same idea more effectively with an active sentence. The following exercises provide practice in changing passive to active sentences. To make a passive sentence active, reverse the procedure that you used with the previous exercises:

Step 1. Make the person or thing that actually performs the action (found after the preposition *by* near the end of the passive sentence) the subject of the active sentence. Omit *by*.

Step 2. Write the main verb in a form that agrees in number with the new subject and has the tense of the form of *be* in the passive sentence. Omit the form of *be*.

Step 3. Make the subject of the passive sentence the object in the active sentence.

Try this sample exercise.

Sample Exercise

Rewrite this passive sentence as an active sentence.

> Jet planes were flown by my brother.

Answer Explanation

Step 1. The person who performed the action (*my brother*) becomes the subject in the active sentence.

> My brother

Step 2. The verb must be past tense since the form of *be* in the passive sentence is *were*, which is a past tense verb.

> My brother flew

Step 3. The subject of the passive sentence (*jet planes*) becomes the object of the active sentence.

> My brother flew jet planes.

Use the same steps with the following exercise.

Exercise

Rewrite this passive sentence in active form.

> My sweater was borrowed by Cindy.

Many sentences contain adverbs and prepositional phrases presenting information on when, where, why, or how an action occurred. Here is an example.

> Your car is *often* driven by Ben *to New Jersey*.
>   ↑   ‿‿‿‿‿‿‿‿‿‿‿
>   adverb   prepositional phrase

Such adverbs and prepositional phrases do not prevent you from transforming a sentence from passive to active form. Here is the above sentence with the adverb and prepositional phrase omitted.

> Your car is driven by Ben.

Before reading further transform the above sentence to active form.

Answer Explanation

> Step 1. The person who performed the action (*Ben*) becomes the subject in the active sentence.

> Ben

> Step 2. The verb must be present tense since the form of *be* in the passive sentence is *is*, which is a present tense verb. It also must be singular, since the new subject (*Ben*) is singular. The main verb in the passive sentence is *driven*, and its singular present tense form is *drives*.

> Ben drives

> Step 3. The subject of the passive sentence (*your car*) becomes the object of the active sentence.

> Ben drives your car.

The adverb and prepositional phrase from the passive form can now be added to this active sentence. The prepositional phrase fits well at the end, and the adverb fits well between the subject and the verb.

> Ben *often* drives your car *to New Jersey*.

Exercise

Rewrite this passive sentence in active form.

> The first Thanksgiving was celebrated by the Pilgrims in 1621, after a bountiful fall harvest.

There are several reasons for occasionally using a passive sentence. You may want to emphasize the person or thing that received the action. Compare these sentences.

> Active: The mother lion rejected the cub.
> Passive: The lion cub was rejected by its mother.

The passive sentence gives more emphasis to the lion cub. If the paper or article that you are writing is mainly concerned with the lion cub, then the passive sentence may be appropriate.

You may also use a passive sentence if doing so provides a better tie-in with the previous sentence. For example, consider these sentences.

We have been feeding this lion cub with a bottle.
The cub was rejected by its mother.

The second sentence is passive. But by beginning with *the cub*, it ties in smoothly with the previous sentence.

Finally, you may use a passive sentence if the person or thing that performed the action is unknown, unimportant, or obvious. Compare these sentences.

Active: Someone stole my car last night.

Passive: My car was stolen last night.

The above passive sentence omits the person who performed the action because the person is unknown. Instead, it emphasizes the object that received the action (*car*).

In the following exercises, you will transform active sentences into passive sentences that do not mention the person who performed the action. Try this sample exercise.

Sample Exercise

Transform this sentence into a passive sentence that does not mention the person who performed the action.

Someone broke the window between midnight and 7 a.m.

Answer Explanation

Step 1. The object of the active sentence is *the window*. It becomes the subject of the passive sentence.

The window

Step 2. Since the new subject is singular, and the verb in the original sentence (*broke*) is past tense, *was* is the appropriate form of *be*.

The window was

Step 3. The past participle form of *broke* is *broken*.

The window was broken

Step 4. The adverbial prepositional phrase telling when the action took place (*between midnight and 7 a.m.*) is added at the end.

The window was broken between midnight and 7 a.m.

Note that the phrase referring to the actor (*by someone*) has been omitted.

Exercise

Rewrite this sentence as a passive sentence that does not mention the person who performed the action.

Jim spilled wine on your white carpet during the party.

Most sentences contain more than just a simple subject, a verb, and a simple object. For example, the subject of the next sentence is a noun modified by a prepositional phrase, and the object is a compound object.

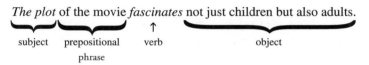

subject	prepositional	verb	object
	phrase		

When a sentence is transformed from active to passive or vice versa, the complete subject and object are moved to the new positions. Try this sample exercise before reading the answer below.

Sample Exercise

Rewrite this sentence in passive form.

The plot of the novel fascinates not just children but also adults.

Don't cheat! Try the exercise before reading the answer.

Answer Explanation

Step 1. The object of the active sentence is *not just children but also adults*. It becomes the subject of the passive sentence.

Not just children but also adults

Step 2. Since the verb in the original sentence is present tense, the form of *be* must also be present tense. And since the new subject is plural, the appropriate form of *be* is *are*.

Not just children but also adults are

Step 3. The past participle of *fascinate* is *fascinated*.

Not just children but also adults are fascinated

Step 4. The subject of the active sentence is placed at the end, preceded by the word *by*.

Not just children but also adults are fascinated by the plot of the movie.

Exercise

Rewrite this sentence in active form.

> The team record for points scored in one game was broken last night by Charles Jackson, who is only a sophomore.

When teachers grade student papers, they sometimes write notes on the papers such as, "Change this sentence to the active voice," or "Avoid weak passive constructions." Unfortunately, most students have little or no understanding of voice, so such comments can be more frustrating than helpful.

However, once students have been taught voice effectively, so that they recognize passive sentences, particularly their longer and often weaker verb phrases, another way of drawing attention to voice is possible. Students could be asked to reread their papers, make a note of each passive sentence (perhaps writing *pass* in the margin), and then decide whether they want to keep the passive or rewrite the sentence in the active voice. This activity would be an excellent way to reinforce the workbook lessons on voice and would ensure that the lessons generalized to student writing. Of course, teachers could still point out passive sentences that might be recast in the active voice. But students who understood voice could fully appreciate, evaluate, and benefit from these suggestions.

CHAPTER
16

DO, EMPHASIS, AND QUESTIONS

As explained earlier, traditional grammar texts frequently provide just a brief explanation of verbs before presenting students with a set of sentences and the instructions to underline the verbs. The set of sentences often includes a question, such as this one.

Are Kevin and Jerome recording their new CD today?

Students are supposed to underline both *are* and *recording* because together they form the verb phrase in the question. But why is the verb phrase split? Why are the two parts separated by the compound subject *Kevin and Jerome*? One of the authors (Whimbey) who learned grammar only after reaching adulthood, remembers that although he could write questions, he never realized that some questions start with part of a verb phrase until this fact was pointed out in a text on transformational grammar. Such "unconscious knowledge" is not unique to grammar. A great deal of learned behavior is not directly available to the conscious mind. Many people can type without looking at the keyboard. Yet they cannot tell someone where the keys for the various letters are located on the keyboard. If given a diagram of a keyboard without the letters labeled, they could not point to the *p*, *r*, and *b* keys without thinking of typing each letter and noting where their fingers move. The knowledge is "in the action," so to speak. The same situation is seen when a father tries to teach his son to tie the knot in a necktie. Although the father may have put a tie on thousands of times, he usually cannot describe how to tie the knot but must demonstrate the procedure. Often a father cannot even tie his son's knot because he is unaccustomed to tying the knot of a necktie he is facing. So he and his son stand in front of a mirror, and the son follows every move that the father "instinctively" makes.

Much of a person's knowledge about his or her native language is of a similar nature. People can often write various types of sentences without consciously knowing the general pattern for each type of sentence. Linguists refer to such knowledge about sentence patterns as "unconscious grammar."

Mentally creating a question to obtain some information is for most people a remarkable example of using unconscious grammar. For instance, most people who have not studied grammar do not consciously know that the verb *do* plays a major role in many of the questions they themselves create. When shown the role that *do* plays in their own questions, they are generally quite amazed. The P-C chapter dealing with *do* and with questions makes students aware of this body of unconscious knowledge, while also helping them avoid common errors and recognize the main verbs of sentences. Here is how the chapter begins.

> This chapter is about the verb *do* and about constructing questions. *Do* is a useful main verb. But it is also an essential helping verb for emphasizing ideas and asking questions. We will begin by reviewing the correct usage of the four forms of *do*: *do*, *does*, *did*, and *done*.
>
> The verb *do* has two present tense forms: *do* and *does*.
>
> ### Present Tense Forms of DO
>
> | Singular Subject Except You or I | Plural Subject And You or I |
> |:---:|:---:|
> | does | do |
>
> In the following sentence, *do* is used as a main verb meaning "perform."

The subject is plural (*scientists*) so the verb is also plural (*do*).

> Medical scientists *do* research on curing diseases.

In the next sentence, the subject is singular, so the singular form of *do* (*does*) is required.

> A medical scientist *does* research on curing diseases.

Inexperienced writers sometimes use the plural form of *do* with a singular subject. For example, the following sentence is incorrect.

> Wrong: Jerry *do* the best he can in school.

Since the subject (*Jerry*) is singular, the singular verb (*does*) is needed.

> Correct: Jerry *does* the best he can in school.

Inexperienced writers also make the opposite error. They use the singular form *does* with a plural subject. The next sentence is incorrect.

> Wrong: The kids *does* the dishes every night.

Because the subject is plural (*kids*), the plural verb (*do*) is required.

> Correct: The kids *do* the dishes every night.

Exercises

Rewrite each sentence with the correct present tense form of *do* in the blank.

1. Pearlene_____ her cardiovascular exercises in the morning.

2. Winter storms _____ so much damage that we spend a week each spring just making repairs.

When the subject of a sentence is *you* or *I*, *do* not *does* is the correct present tense verb. A common error is to use *does* when the subject is *you* or *I*. The following sentences are incorrect.

> Wrong: I *does* my best.
> Wrong: You *does* your best.

Both sentences should use *do*.

> Correct: I *do* my best.
> Correct: You *do* your best.

Sample Exercise

The following sentence contains two blank spaces. *Do* belongs in one space and *does* belongs in the other. Rewrite the sentence with the correct verbs in the blanks.

Tony _____ the cleaning, and I _____ the shopping.

Answer Explanation

This sentence contains two clauses connected with the conjunction *and*. Here are the two clauses.

Tony_____the cleaning.
I_____the shopping.

In the first clause, the subject is *Tony*, so the verb should be *does*. In the second clause, the subject is *I*, so the verb should be *do*.

Tony *does* the cleaning, and I *do* the shopping.

Exercises

Each sentence is composed of two clauses, with a blank in each clause. Rewrite the sentence with *do* in one blank and *does* in the other.

1. Because you _____ me so many favors, and your husband _____ so much for me also, I want to take you both to dinner this Saturday.
2. Sometimes John _____ the laundry and I _____ the ironing, while other times we reverse roles.

The past tense form of the verb *do* is *did*. *Did* is the correct past tense form for all subjects—singular and plural subjects as well as *you* and *I*. Never use *done* as the past tense form of *do*.

Exercise

Rewrite this sentence with the present tense form of *do* changed to the past tense form (*did*).

The company does a brisk business seven days a week.

In Chapter 14 you formed the present perfect tense with forms of the helping verb *have*. You followed the form of *have* with the past participle of the main verb. The past participle of the verb *do* is *done*.

Base Verb	Past Tense	Past Participle
do	did	done

In the exercises below, you will form the present perfect tense for sentences in which a form of *do* is the main verb. Try this sample exercise.

Sample Exercise

Rewrite this sentence with the underlined verb in the present perfect tense.

I <u>did</u> the assignment and have turned it in.

Answer Explanation

The appropriate form of *have* for the subject *I* is *have*. The past participle form of *do* is *done*. Here is the answer.

I *have done* the assignment and have turned it in.

Note that it would be incorrect to use the past participle *done* in this sentence without a form of *have*.

Wrong: I *done* the assignment and have turned it in.

Only use *done* when a past participle is appropriate. *Done* is not the past tense of *do*.

Exercises

Rewrite each sentence in the present perfect tense.

1. Marty did our yardwork since we moved here.
2. Leonard and Sylvia did their laundry at this laundromat every Thursday for the past three years.

Do can be used as a helping verb to make a statement emphatic (stronger) and to emphasize that it is true. Compare these sentences.

Marcus *brushed* his teeth.

Marcus *did brush* his teeth.

The second sentence makes the statement stronger. It emphasizes the truth or accuracy of the statement.

The second sentence uses the past tense form *did* because the first sentence contains the past tense form *brushed*. Note that in the second sentence, *did* is inserted right before the main verb (*brush*).

Note also that when *did* is inserted before the main verb, the base form of the main verb is used (*brush*). Recall from a previous chapter that when a modal like *can* or *must* is inserted before a verb, the verb always takes its base form. The same is true when *do* is inserted before a verb. Try this sample exercise.

Sample Exercise

Rewrite the following sentence so that it makes an emphatic statement by inserting *did* before the main verb. Remember to change the main verb to its base form.

> Leslie *drove* a race car several years ago.

Answer Explanation

Did must be inserted before the main verb to make the statement emphatic. Also, the main verb (*drove*) must be changed to its base form (*drive*).

> Leslie *did drive* a race car several years ago.

Exercise

Rewrite the following sentence so that it makes an emphatic statement by inserting *did* before the main verb.

> Marva paid the telephone bill.

Do or *does* can be used to make a present tense sentence emphatic. Here is an example.

> Ronda *brushes* her teeth regularly.
>
> Ronda *does brush* her teeth regularly.

Whether *do* or *does* should be used depends on the subject of the sentence. In the above example, the subject (*Ronda*) is singular, so *does* is used. In the next example, the subject (*children*) is plural, so *do* is used.

> The children *brush* their teeth regularly.
>
> The children *do brush* their teeth regularly.

Finally, if the subject is *you* or *I*, the form *do* is used.

> I *brush* my teeth regularly.
>
> I *do brush* my teeth regularly.

Note that whether *do* or *does* is inserted before the main verb, the main verb takes its base form. In all three of the above examples, when a form of *do* is inserted, the main verb takes the base form *brush*.

Exercises

Rewrite each sentence with *do* or *does* inserted before the main verb and with the verb in its base form.

1. Our children play with your son.
2. Your son plays with our children.

3. I love your singing.

4. You eat more than your share of everything.

Let us now turn our attention to constructing questions. We will deal with two types of questions: those that can be answered with yes or no; and those that ask for more information. First we will discuss yes/no questions because they are easier to construct and they form the basis for constructing many other questions.

If a simple sentence contains *is*, *are*, *was*, *were*, or *am* as a main verb or helping verb, moving that word to the front of the sentence will turn the sentence into a question. The only other thing you need to do is place a question mark at the end of the question.

Here is a sentence with *is* as the main verb.

Mr. Jackson *is* your new football coach.

To create a question from this sentence, simply move *is* to the front and put a question mark at the end.

Is Mr. Jackson your new football coach?

Try this sample exercise.

Sample Exercise

Create a question from this sentence.

Kevin and Jerome are recording their new CD today.

Answer Explanation

To create a question from this sentence, *are* must be moved to the front and a question mark must be placed at the end.

Are Kevin and Jerome *recording* their new CD today?

Exercises

Create a question from each sentence.

1. Mary is going to retire this year.

2. Your dogs were restless during the thunderstorm.

If a simple sentence contains a helping verb, moving the helping verb to the beginning of the sentence turns the sentence into a question. In addition to forms of *be*, helping verbs include forms of *have*, forms of *do*, and modals (*can*, *could*, *will*, *would*, *should*, *may*, *might*, and *must*). Try this sample exercise.

Sample Exercise

Create a question from this sentence.

> We can go to the football game this weekend.

Answer Explanation

This sentence contains the modal *can* as a helping verb in the verb phrase *can go*. To create a question, *can* is moved to the front and a question mark is placed at the end.

> Can we go to the football game this weekend?

Exercises

Create a question from each sentence.

1. Ron will take some college courses this summer.
2. Raphael may borrow this book for the weekend.

If a sentence does not contain *be* as a main verb, and it does not contain a helping verb, then a form of *do* must be added to create a yes/no question. Consider this sentence.

> Selina *likes* mushrooms.

In modern English you cannot create a question by just moving the verb *likes* to the front of the sentence, although you could in the English of Shakespeare's time.

> Wrong: *likes* Selina mushrooms?

Instead, you must first add a form of *do* to the sentence.

> Selina *does* like mushrooms.

You know that this is called the emphatic form of the sentence because it emphasizes the statement. You create a question from this emphatic sentence by moving *does* to the front.

> *Does* Selina like mushrooms?

Here is a sample exercise.

Sample Exercise

Create a question from this sentence.

> Phil went to work this morning.

Answer Explanation

Step 1. The verb in this sentence is a past tense form (*went*). Therefore, the form of *do* that must be added to create an emphatic sentence is *did*. The main verb (*went*) takes its base form (*go*).

> Phil *did go* to work this morning.

Step 2. A question is created by moving *did* to the front and adding a question mark at the end.

> *Did* Phil go to work this morning?

Exercises

Create a question from each sentence.

1. Students like the new math teacher.
2. Jack ate two whole pizzas again last night.
3. The next plane to Puerto Rico leaves at 1:05 P.M.

Let us now consider questions that request more information than just yes or no. These questions often begin with *who, what, why, which, when, where,* or *how.* Note that all the words except *how* begin with *wh.* Therefore, grammarians call them *wh*-words. To create a question about the subject of a sentence, the subject is replaced by the appropriate *wh*-word. The appropriate *wh*-word for information about the subject is usually *who, what,* or *which.* Consider this sentence.

> Lenny baked those delicious chocolate chip cookies.

If you did not know who baked the cookies, you could form a question by simply substituting *who* for *Lenny* in the sentence.

> *Who* baked those delicious chocolate chip cookies?

Try this sample exercise.

Sample Exercise

Write a question by replacing the underlined subject of the following sentence with *what* and placing a question mark at the end.

> *Greed* has been the cause of many wars.

Answer Explanation

The word *greed* is replaced by *what.* A question mark is added at the end.

> *What* has been the cause of many wars?

Exercises

In each exercise write a question by replacing the underlined subject of the sentence with the suggested *wh*-word and placing a question mark at the end.

1. Replace the underlined subject with *which*.

   Jupiter is the largest planet in the solar system.

2. Replace the underlined subject with *who*.

   The ancient Greeks believed that Atlas held the earth on his shoulders.

3. Replace the underlined subject with *what*.

   The Governor of New York's stolen Corvette was found abandoned in Chicago.

To ask a question about information that is not found in the subject of a sentence, a *wh*-word replaces a word or phrase in another position in the sentence. Consider this sentence.

Julia has been living *in Detroit* for the past three years.

Suppose we do not know where Julia has been living. We want to transform the sentence into a question for getting this information. We might try replacing *in Detroit* with *where*.

Julia has been living *where* for the past three years

The above sentence could be used as a question in some contexts, such as asking someone to repeat the information. But it is not the standard form of a question. Suppose we move *where* to the front.

where Julia has been living for the past three years

This sounds somewhat like a question, but it is still not the correct form for a question. However, suppose we go back to the original sentence and first transform it into a yes/no question by moving *has* to the front.

Has Julia been living *in Detroit* for the past three years?

Now we replace *in Detroit* with *where*.

has Julia been living *where* for the past three years

Finally, we move *where* to the front.

Where has Julia been living for the past three years?

In the following exercises you will start with yes/no questions and transform them into questions asking for more information. Try this sample exercise.

Sample Exercise

Rewrite this yes/no question as a question asking for more information by replacing the underlined words with *when* and then moving *when* to the front.

> Will Cindy leave for college <u>next Tuesday</u>?

Answer Explanation

Step 1. The underlined words are replaced with *when*.

> will Cindy leave for college *when*

Step 2. *When* is moved to the front.

> *When* will Cindy leave for college?

Exercises

Each exercise presents a yes/no question. Rewrite the yes/no question as a question asking for more information by replacing the underlined word(s) with the suggested *wh*-word and then moving the *wh*-word to the front.

1. Replace the underlined word with *what*.

   Should we have <u>enchiladas</u> for lunch?

2. Replace the underlined words with *why*.

   Is Vicki spending the summer in Madrid <u>to learn Spanish</u>?

In the last set of exercises you transformed yes/no questions to *wh*-word questions. In the next exercises you will transform regular sentences to *wh*-word questions. To do this, you will first transform each sentence into a yes/no question. Then you will transform the yes/no question into a *wh*-word question. Try the following sample exercise before reading the answer below.

Sample Exercise

Rewrite this sentence as a yes/no question by moving *were* to the front. Then rewrite the yes/no question as a *wh*-word question by replacing the underlined words with *where* and moving *where* to the front.

> Fiberglass cows were popular <u>in Chicago</u> last summer.

Answer Explanation

Step 1. Move *were* to the front.

Were fiberglass cows popular <u>in Chicago</u> last summer?

Step 2. Replace *in Chicago* with *where*.

were fiberglass cows popular *where* last summer

Step 3. Move *where* to the front.

Where were fiberglass cows popular last summer?

Exercises

Rewrite each sentence as a question with the underlined words replaced by the suggested *wh*-word.

1. Replace the underlined words with *why*.

   Goggles are required in shop class <u>to prevent eye injuries</u>.

2. Replace the underlined words with *where*.

   Donna is going <u>to Disney World</u> next summer.

3. Replace the underlined words with *when*.

   Donna is going to Disney World <u>next summer</u>.

4. Replace the underlined words with *what*.

   The landlord will install <u>a new heater</u> in our house next week.

In the last set of exercises, the sentences contained a helping verb or a form of *be* as a main verb. Therefore, it was not necessary to add a form of *do* before transforming the sentence into a yes/no question. However, in the next set of exercises, you will have to add a form of *do*. Consider this sentence.

Margarita found a diamond ring in a can of beans.

Suppose we do not know where Margarita found the ring. We want to transform the sentence into a question about where the ring was found. First we must add a form of *do* in front of the main verb (*found*) and change the main verb to its base form (*find*). Since *found* is a past tense verb, the form of *do* we add is *did*.

Margarita *did* find a diamond ring in a can of beans.

Next we move *did* to the front to form a yes/no question.

did Margarita find a diamond ring in a can of beans

Then we replace *in a can of beans* with *where*.

did Margarita find a diamond ring *where*

Finally, we move *where* to the front.

Where did Margarita find a diamond ring?

Exercises

Rewrite each sentence as a question with the underlined words replaced by the suggested *wh*-word.

1. Replace the underlined words with *how*.

   Ski resorts increase the amount of snow on their slopes <u>by using snow-making machines</u>.

2. Replace the underlined words with *when*.

   Mary graduated from college <u>in 1995</u>.

3. Replace the underlined words with *what*.

   Arnold gave his wife <u>a diamond bracelet</u> for her birthday.

4. Replace the underlined words with *why*.

   Jane left work early <u>because her son got sick at school</u>.

5. Replace the underlined words with *how*.

   Your cousin Tim went to New York <u>by bus</u>.

Early transformational grammarians believed that when a person wanted to ask a question, he or she began with a sentence and then transformed it into a question, much as we do in the above exercises. Most modern grammarians no longer hold this view. Nevertheless, students find the exercises fascinating in revealing the relationship between regular sentences and questions, as well as the unconscious knowledge that they possess which allows them to create questions. While the chapter on constructing questions may be the least useful for directly improving students' writing skills, it may be the one that impresses student most with how interesting grammar can be in highlighting the amazing power of the human mind to use language.

CHAPTER
17

NOUN CLAUSES

O ne of the topics in grammar that students enjoy most is noun clauses. Here is a sentence with an underlined noun clause.

That too much sugar makes her daughter hyperactive was obvious to Leslie.

The underlined material is called a noun clause because (1) it consists of an entire clause, including a subject (*sugar*) and a verb (*makes*); and (2) it is used in a noun position in the overall sentence, namely the subject position.

Students enjoy learning about noun clauses because with a little practice, noun clauses are easy to construct; yet they allow a person to create rich sentences that impress a reader with the verbal skills of the writer.

There are two types of noun clauses, those which begin with *that*, and those which begin with *wh*-words. Noun clauses which begin with *that* are easier to construct, so the P-C workbook begins with them:

You know that the subject of a sentence is generally a noun, as in this sentence.

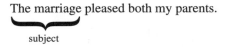

The marriage pleased both my parents.

subject

However, here is a sentence which has an entire clause for a subject.

clause

That Flo married Barry pleased both my parents.

subject

You can see that the clause in this sentence is playing the same role as the noun *marriage* in the above sentence. Both are playing the role of the subject and both are followed by the same verb (*pleased*).

Recall that a clause is a group of words containing a subject and a verb. Here is a clause.

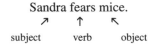

Sandra fears mice.

subject   verb   object

An independent clause can stand alone as a sentence. The above clause is an independent clause. However, a dependent clause may contain an extra word that prevents it from standing alone. The word *that* prevents the following clause from standing alone.

that Sandra fears mice

However, this dependent clause can serve as the subject of a larger sentence:

That Sandra fears mice amuses her brother.

subject

A clause playing a role usually played by a noun is called a "noun clause." One way to create a noun clause is to place the word *that* in front of a clause. You have just seen one example. Here is another.

that + *Miguel won the race* = that Miguel won the race

clause

This noun clause can be used as the subject of a sentence.

That Miguel won the race surprised everyone except Miguel.

Try this sample exercise.

Sample Exercise

Create a noun clause from the second sentence by placing *that* in front. Then rewrite the first sentence with the words NOUN CLAUSE replaced by the noun clause you created.

> NOUN CLAUSE makes my family very happy.
> I will be home from the Navy for Christmas.

Answer Explanation

Step 1. A noun clause is created from the second sentence by writing *that* in front.

> *that* I will be be home from the Navy for Christmas

Step 2. The noun clause is placed in the subject slot of the first sentence.

> *That I will be home from the Navy for Christmas* makes my family very happy.
> verb

Note that the verb in the last sentence is *makes*. This is the singular form of the verb *make*. If the subject of a sentence is a noun clause, then the verb of the main sentence takes the form used for a singular subject.

Exercises

For each exercise, create a noun clause from the second sentence by adding *that* in front. Then rewrite the first sentence with the words NOUN CLAUSE replaced by the noun clause you created.

1. NOUN CLAUSE has been confirmed by biologists.
    Wolves mate for life.

2. NOUN CLAUSE is proven on American highways every night.
    Excessive drinking causes accidents.

The object of a verb is usually a noun. For example, the noun *Tom* is the object in this sentence.

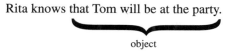

Rita knows Tom.

subject verb object

But sometimes the object of a verb is a noun clause, as in this sentence.

Rita knows that Tom will be at the party.

object

In the last exercises you used noun clauses as subjects of sentences. In the next exercises you will use noun clauses as objects in sentences. Try this sample exercise.

Sample Exercise

Create a noun clause from the second sentence by adding *that* in front. Then rewrite the first sentence with the words NOUN CLAUSE replaced by the noun clause you created.

Helen hopes NOUN CLAUSE.

One of her novels will be made into a movie.

Answer Explanation

Step 1. The second sentence is made into a noun clause by writing *that* in front.

that one of her novels will be made into a movie

Step 2. The noun clause is placed in the object slot of the first sentence.

Helen hopes *that one of her novels will be made into a movie.*

Exercises

For each exercise, create a noun clause from the second sentence by writing *that* in front. Then rewrite the first sentence with the words NOUN CLAUSE replaced by the noun clause you created.

1.   History shows NOUN CLAUSE.

Humans have not learned how to avoid war.

2.   Tammy fears NOUN CLAUSE.

She is catching a cold.

When a noun clause beginning with *that* is the object of a verb, the word *that* may sometimes be deleted. For example, here is the answer to one of the above exercises.

Tammy fears that she is catching a cold.

This sentence can be written without *that*.

Tammy fears she is catching a cold.

However, *that* cannot be deleted if the noun clause is the subject of the sentence. For example, here is the answer to another of the earlier exercises.

That wolves mate for life has been confirmed by biologists.

That cannot be deleted because the noun clause is the subject:

Wrong: Wolves mate for life has been confirmed by biologists.

Also, *that* should not be deleted from the object if doing so could lead to momentary confusion or misinterpretation. Consider this sentence.

Paul thinks that impulsively making decisions is foolish.

Deleting *that* could result in a reader momentarily believing that Paul thinks impulsively.

Paul thinks impulsively. . . .

Therefore, *that* should not be deleted from such a sentence.

Exercise

Rewrite the first sentence with the second sentence used as a noun clause serving as the object of the verb. Omit the connector *that*.

1. Sheila thinks NOUN CLAUSE.

Her cat is a little crazy.

Noun clauses can begin with *wh*-words as well as *that*. You already worked with *wh*-words in the last chapter when you created *wh*-word questions. Creating *wh*-word clauses is easier than creating *wh*-word questions, so you should find the following exercises easy. Nevertheless, the sentence patterns you will be practicing are very useful.

The following sentence uses a noun clause as the object of the verb.

Jack wondered *who ate all the doughnuts.*

subject   verb   object

Here is the noun clause alone.

who ate all the doughnuts

This noun clause was created by substituting *who* for the subject in the following sentence.

Sentence: *Someone* ate all the doughnuts.

Noun Clause: *who* ate all the doughnuts

You know from the last chapter that a *wh*-word can replace other parts of a sentence besides a subject. It can replace an object. It can also replace a word or phrase presenting information about location, time, cause, or manner.

After an appropriate *wh*-word is substituted in a sentence, the *wh*-word is moved to the front in order to form a noun clause. This noun clause can then be used in another sentence. For example, consider these sentences.

NOUN CLAUSE is uncertain.

The hurricane will come ashore *somewhere*.

The appropriate *wh*-word to replace the italicized word in the second sentence is *where*.

the hurricane will come ashore *where*

A noun clause is formed by moving the *wh*-word to the front.

where the hurricane will come ashore

The noun clause can be used as the subject of the first sentence.

Where the hurricane will come ashore is uncertain.

In the exercises below you will create noun clauses with *wh*-words and then use them to fill slots in other sentences. Try this sample exercise.

Sample Exercise

Create a noun clause from the second sentence by substituting *why* for the underlined phrase and then moving *why* to the front. Rewrite the first sentence with that noun clause.

The police wanted to know NOUN CLAUSE.

The office had been left unlocked last night *for some reason*.

Answer Explanation

Step 1. The phrase *for some reason* is replaced by *why*.

the office had been left unlocked last night *why*

138

Step 2. *Why* is moved to the front of the clause.

Noun Clause: *why* the office had been left unlocked last night

Step 3. The first sentence is rewritten with this noun clause.

The police wanted to know *why the office had been left unlocked last night.*

Exercises

In each exercise, create a noun clause from the second sentence by substituting the suggested *wh*-word for the underlined word or phrase and moving the *wh*-word to the front. Then rewrite the first sentence with the noun clause.

1. Replace *something* with *what.*

    The janitor does not know NOUN CLAUSE.

    Something is clogging the drain in the shower.

2. Replace *something* with *what.*

    NOUN CLAUSE is the topic for discussion at the next city council meeting.

    Something can be done to reduce crime.

3. Replace *somewhere* with *where.*

    Debra has not thought about NOUN CLAUSE.

    She will go somewhere on vacation this summer.

4. Replace *for a reason* with *why.*

    Many homeowners attending the meeting wanted to know NOUN CLAUSE.

    Their property taxes had been raised for a reason.

5. Replace *sometime* with *when.*

    The head of marketing has been asking me NOUN CLAUSE.

    My report on the South American markets for our products will be completed sometime.

6. Replace *somehow* with *how.*

    George wondered NOUN CLAUSE.

    The magician somehow thrust swords through the box without injuring his partner locked inside.

7. Replace *someone* with *who.*

    The principal already knows NOUN CLAUSE.

    Someone won the scholarship to study art in France this summer.

8. Replace *some* with *which*.

    Tomorrow our coach is going to decide NOUN CLAUSE.

    <u>Some</u> players will travel with the team to Detroit.

For the remaining exercises, you decide which *wh*-word should replace the underlined word in the second sentence. Then rewrite the first sentence with the noun clause you create from the second sentence.

9. I wonder NOUN CLAUSE.

    <u>Someone</u> lives in that beautiful house.

10. The fire investigator discovered NOUN CLAUSE.

    <u>Something</u> caused the fire.

Many of the exercises in the P-C workbook show students how a modern linguist might analyze a complex sentence. For example, here is the answer for the last exercise.

The fire investigator discovered what caused the fire.

A linguist would analyze this sentence into the *two* sentences presented in the exercise and would describe the transformations that the students made in getting the answer. Thus, in addition to teaching grammar and writing skills, such exercises provide a practical introduction to the science of modern linguistics.

Students must be familiar with advanced grammatical structures such as noun clauses in order to fully understand verb usage. For example, in the following sentence, the subject is a clause and therefore requires a singular verb (*has*).

That wolves mate for life has been confirmed by biologists.

noun clause   singular verb

But a student who lacks a firm understanding of such constructions could easily make the mistake of thinking that the plural noun *wolves* is the subject and that the verb should take the plural form *have*.

Wrong: That wolves mate for life *have* been confirmed by biologists.

However, a student who has added noun clauses to sentences recognizes that *wolves* is the subject of the noun clause. Therefore, its verb (*mate*) is plural, but the verb for the entire sentence must be singular.

Most students enjoy studying noun clauses because when they are taught effectively, students quickly learn how to use them and soon begin to feel proud of the interesting sentences they can create.

CHAPTER
18

ENRICHING SENTENCES WITH VERBALS: A BONUS FOR UNDERSTANDING VERBS

V erbals are words that have their origin in verbs but are not used as verbs. There are three types of verbals: gerunds, participles, and infinitives. While verbals look like forms of verbs, they play different roles in sentences. Participles act somewhat like adjectives, and gerunds act somewhat like nouns. Infinitives are more versatile and can act like nouns, adjectives, or adverbs. Verbals are fairly advanced grammatical structures: Students who have suffered through *traditional* grammar year after year, while understanding little of it, have been totally confused by verbals. Therefore, they are pleasantly surprised when they are taught with the P-C Approach and find themselves using verbals to create rich, informative sentences. The P-C Approach begins with gerunds because they are easiest to use:

Gerunds: Verbals in Noun Slots

The *ing* form of a verb can be used as a noun. For example, compare these sentences.

> *Food* is not expensive.
> ↗
> subject
> ↘
> *Eating* is not expensive.

The word *food* in the first sentence is a noun. Food is a class of physical objects. The sentence makes a statement about these physical objects. But sometimes you want to make a statement about an activity. The second sentence makes a statement about eating. The word *eating* is the subject of the sentence. Since the subject of a sentence is usually a noun, the word *eating* in the second sentence plays the role of a noun. However, the word *eating* is the *ing* form of the verb *eat*. When the *ing* form of a verb is used as a noun, it is given a special name: It is called a "gerund."

In the following exercises, you will write sentences that have gerunds as subjects. Consider this sentence.

> GERUND burns calories.
> ↗   ↑   ↖
> subject   verb   object

The above sentence has the word GERUND in the subject position. We will create a gerund from the verb in another sentence and then replace the word GERUND with an actual gerund.

We can create a gerund from the verb in the next sentence.

> People swim.

A gerund is created from the verb in this sentence by changing it to its *ing* form. Here is the *ing* form of *swim*.

> Gerund: swimming

We can now replace the word GERUND with *swimming* in the sentence above.

> GERUND burns calories.
>
> *Swimming* burns calories.

Try this sample exercise.

Sample Exercise

Create a gerund from the verb in the second sentence. Then rewrite the first sentence with the gerund used as the subject.

GERUND is educational and enjoyable.
People *read*.

Answer Explanation

Step 1. A gerund is created from the verb in the second sentence (*read*) by changing it to its *ing* form. The *ing* form of *read* is *reading*.

Gerund: reading

Step 2. The gerund is placed in the subject slot of the first sentence.

Reading is educational and enjoyable.

Exercises

In each exercise, create a gerund from the verb in the second sentence. Then rewrite the first sentence with the gerund used as its subject.

1. GERUND can help a tense person relax.

   People laugh.

2. GERUND is a rewarding profession.

   People teach.

You know that a verb can have objects and modifiers. Since a gerund is derived from a verb, it too can have objects and modifiers. Here are two examples.

A gerund along with its modifiers and/or objects is called a gerund phrase.

<u>Gerund Phrases</u>
eating quickly
loving beauty

A gerund phrase can be used as the subject of a sentence. Here is a sentence with the words GERUND PHRASE in the subject position.

GERUND PHRASE causes indigestion.

subject

We can replace the words GERUND PHRASE with an actual gerund phrase (*eating quickly*).

Eating quickly causes indigestion.

subject

In the following exercises, you will be presented with two sentences. One sentence will have the words GERUND PHRASE in the subject position.

GERUND PHRASE is an investment in the future of humanity.

subject

People teach children to read.

You will create a gerund phrase from the second sentence and then use it to replace the words GERUND PHRASE. Consider this sentence.

People teach children to read.

To create a gerund phrase from this sentence, we begin with the *ing* form of the verb *teach*. The *ing* form of *teach* is *teaching*.

Gerund: teaching

The gerund phrase consists of the gerund (*teaching*) and everything that follows the verb in the above sentence (*children to read*).

Gerund Phrase: teaching children to read

This gerund phrase can be made the subject of a sentence by letting it replace the words GERUND PHRASE:

GERUND PHRASE is an investment in the future of humanity.

Teaching children to read is an investment in the future of humanity.

subject

Try this sample exercise.

Sample Exercise

Create a gerund phrase from the second sentence. Then rewrite the first sentence with the gerund phrase used as the subject.

GERUND PHRASE is forbidden by international law.
People hunt certain species of whales.

146

Answer Explanation

Step 1. A gerund is created from the second sentence by changing the verb to its *ing* form. The *ing* form of *hunt* is *hunting*.

  Gerund: hunting

Step 2. The gerund phrase includes the gerund (*hunting*) and everything that follows the verb in the above sentence (*certain species of whales*).

  Gerund Phrase: hunting certain species of whales

Step 3. This gerund phrase replaces the words GERUND PHRASE in the first sentence.

  GERUND PHRASE is forbidden by international law.

  Hunting certain species of whales is forbidden by international law.

The gerund phrase is now the subject of the sentence.

Exercise

Create a gerund phrase from the second sentence. Then rewrite the first sentence with the gerund phrase used as the subject.

  GERUND PHRASE is pleasant exercise.

  People jog through the park.

The object of a verb is generally a noun. For example, the object in the following sentence is the noun *chocolate*.

  Harry likes *chocolate*.

  subject   verb   object

However, the object of a verb can also be a gerund phrase. Here is a sentence with the words GERUND PHRASE occupying the position for the object.

  Betty likes GERUND PHRASE.

  subject   verb   object

We can replace the words GERUND PHRASE with an actual gerund phrase (*Sailing on a lake*).

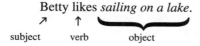

  Betty likes *sailing on a lake*.

  subject   verb   object

In the following exercises, you will create a gerund phrase from one sentence. You will then use that gerund phrase as the object in another sentence. Try this sample exercise.

Sample Exercise

Create a gerund phrase from the second sentence. Then rewrite the first sentence with the gerund phrase used as the object.

> Stan avoids GERUND PHRASE.
>
> People drive home in rush-hour traffic.

Answer Explanation

Step 1. A gerund is created from the verb in the second sentence by changing it to its *ing* form. The *ing* form of *drive* is *driving*. Here is the gerund phrase.

> driving home in rush-hour traffic

Step 2. The gerund phrase is placed in the object slot of the first sentence.

> Stan avoids *driving home in rush-hour traffic*.

Exercise

Create a gerund phrase from the second sentence. Then rewrite the first sentence with the gerund phrase used as the object.

> I really hated GERUND PHRASE.
>
> I walked to school on cold mornings in Wisconsin.

Usually the object of a preposition is a noun, as in this sentence.

> The booklet is about *dogs*.
>   ↗   ↖
>   preposition   object of preposition

The noun *dogs* is the object of the preposition *about*.

But in the next sentence, the object of the preposition is a gerund phrase.

> The booklet is about *choosing a dog*.
>   ↗   ⎵⎵⎵⎵⎵⎵
>   preposition   object of preposition

The gerund phrase *choosing a dog* is the object of the preposition *about*.

In the following exercises, you will create a gerund phrase from one sentence. You will then use that gerund phrase as the object of a preposition in another sentence. Try this sample exercise.

Sample Exercise

Create a gerund phrase from the second sentence. Then rewrite the first sentence with the gerund phrase used as the object of the preposition *by*.

> Our quarterback won the game by <u>GERUND PHRASE</u>.
>
> He threw a last-minute touchdown pass.

Answer Explanation

Step 1. A gerund is created from the verb in the second sentence by changing it to its *ing* form. The *ing* form of *threw* is *throwing*. Here is the gerund phrase.

> throwing a last-minute touchdown pass

Step 2. The gerund phrase is placed in the slot after the preposition *by* in the first sentence.

> Our quarterback won the game by *throwing a last-minute touchdown pass.*

Exercises

In each exercise, create a gerund phrase from the second sentence. Then rewrite the first sentence with the gerund phrase used as the object of a preposition.

1. Mark Twain was a journalist for many years before GERUND PHRASE.

    Mark Twain became a bestselling novelist.

2. After GERUND PHRASE, Phil had a painful sunburn.

    Phil spent the whole day at the beach.

Participles: Verbals That Act as Adjectives

Participles are forms of verbs that can be used to modify nouns. Recall that a passive sentence uses the past participle form of a verb. Here is an example.

> The building was *abandoned* by its owner.
>
>   ↗
>
>   past participle

The person performing the action may be deleted from the sentence.

> The building was abandoned.

Note in the above sentence that *abandoned* describes the building. It provides information about the building. *Abandoned* is playing the role of an adjective. Therefore, *abandoned* can now be used to modify the noun *building* in another sentence about the same building, such as this sentence:

> The *building* was renovated by the city.

The past participle (*abandoned*) is inserted right before the noun it modifies (*building*).

> The *abandoned* building was renovated by the city.

Try this sample exercise.

Sample Exercise

Rewrite the first sentence with the past participle from the second sentence inserted right before the noun it modifies.

> A friend went with Jim to the lawyer's office.

> The friend is trusted.

Answer Explanation

The past participial in the second sentence is *trusted*. It modifies *friend*, so it is placed before *friend* in the first sentence.

> A *trusted* friend went with Jim to the lawyer's office.

Exercises

In each exercise, rewrite the first sentence with the past participle from the second sentence inserted right before the noun it modifies.

1. The tea was refreshing after our long hike.

    The tea was iced.

2. Skiing carelessly leads to bones.

    The bones are broken.

3. Before antibiotics were developed, many soldiers died from wounds.

    The wounds were infected.

In a passive sentence, the past participle is often followed by adverbs and prepositional phrases. For example, in the next sentence the participle *destroyed* is followed by the prepositional phrase *by fire*.

> The house was *destroyed by fire*.

The phrase *destroyed by fire* is a participial phrase. A participial phrase can be inserted after a noun to modify it. Consider these sentences.

150

> The house was fully insured.
> The house was destroyed by fire.

The word *destroyed* in the second sentence is a past participle. *Destroyed* and the words that follow it in the second sentence present information about the house.

> The house was <u>destroyed by fire</u>.

This underlined phrase can be used to modify *house* in the other sentence.

> The house *destroyed by fire* was fully insured.

Try this sample exercise.

Sample Exercise

Rewrite the first sentence with the past participial phrase from the second sentence inserted right after the noun it modifies.

> The pictures were painted by Bobby in school.
>
> The pictures are taped on the refrigerator.

Answer Explanation

The underlined words in the sentence below can be used as a participial phrase.

> The pictures are <u>taped on the refrigerator</u>.

The participle phrase is inserted in the first sentence right after the noun it modifies (*pictures*).

> The pictures *taped on the refrigerator* were painted by Bobby in school.

Exercises

In each exercise, rewrite the first sentence with the participial phrase from the second sentence inserted right after the noun it modifies.

1. A car hit three people waiting at a bus stop.

   The car was driven by an uninsured motorist.

2. An Indian warrior is a hero to many Native Americans.

   The warrior was named Crazy Horse.

3. Wilson intercepted the pass.

   The pass was intended for Johnson.

So far we have discussed past participles. Now we turn to present participles. The word *crying* in the following sentence plays the role of an adjective because it modifies the noun *child*.

> The *crying child* is lost.

However, *crying* is the *ing* form of the verb *cry*. It is part of the present progressive verb phrase (*is crying*) in the following sentence.

> The child *is crying*.

When an *ing* form of a verb is used as an adjective, it is called a present participle. Generally a present participle is placed right before the noun it modifies. Consider these sentences.

> The actress greeted her fans.
> The actress was smiling.

In the second sentence, the word *smiling* describes the actress. It can be placed before the word *actress* in the first sentence.

> The *smiling* actress greeted her fans.

In this sentence, *smiling* modifies the noun *actress*.

In the following exercises, you will use present participles to modify nouns. Try this sample exercise.

Sample Exercise

Rewrite the first sentence with the *ing* form of the verb from the second sentence inserted right before the noun it modifies.

> Our team owes its success to our coach.

> The coach is inspiring.

Answer Explanation

The present participle *inspiring* describes the coach. Therefore, it is inserted right before *coach* in the first sentence.

> Our team owes its success to our *inspiring* coach.
> ↗
> present participle modifying *coach*

Exercises

In each exercise, rewrite the first sentence with the present participle (*ing* word) from the second sentence inserted right before the noun it modifies.

1. The heat exhausted the hikers.

    The heat was punishing.

152

2.   The lights at the railroad tracks signaled that a train was near.

     The lights were flashing.

A verb in a sentence is often followed by an adverb, an object, or a prepositional phrase. For example, the progressive verb *carrying* is followed by the object *baby* in this sentence.

> The fireman is *carrying a baby*.

The progressive verb and its object can be used to modify the word *fireman* in the following sentence.

> A *fireman* ran from the burning building.

The phrase *carrying a baby* is inserted right after *fireman*.

> A fireman *carrying a baby* ran from the burning building.

The phrase *carrying a baby* is called a "present participial phrase." Note that it is added right after the noun it modifies. Try this sample exercise.

Sample Exercise

Rewrite the first sentence with the present participial phrase from the second sentence inserted right after the noun it modifies.

> The girl is my niece.
>
> The girl is singing off key.

Answer Explanation

The present participial phrase in the second sentence consists of the participle (*singing*) and the prepositional phrase *off key*.

> The girl is *singing off key*.

This phrase presents information about the girl, so it is inserted right after *girl* in the first sentence.

> The girl *singing off key* is my niece.

Exercises

In each exercise, rewrite the first sentence with the present participial phrase from the second sentence inserted right after the noun it modifies.

1.   The airline passenger looked annoyed.

     The airline passenger was *sitting behind the crying baby*.

2.   The limousine will take the president to the airport.

     The limousine is *entering the parking lot*.

Note: In the next exercise the noun you will modify is at the end of the first sentence. So the participial phrase from the second sentence must be added at the end of the first sentence.

    3.   The park attendant gave a lollipop to a child.

          The child was *crying over his lost puppy*.

An earlier chapter explained the difference between essential and nonessential relative clauses. Participial phrases can also be essential or nonessential. This is true for both past and present participial phrases. If a participial phrase is not essential in identifying the person or thing referred to by the noun it modifies—if it provides only parenthetical or extra information—it is enclosed in commas. Compare these sentences.

    The boy *wearing a dark blue suit* is my brother.

    Senator Bryd, *wearing a dark blue suit*, gave a moving speech.

In the first sentence, the boy is identified by the suit he is wearing. The participial phrase is essential for identifying the boy, so it is not set off in commas. But in the second sentence, the person is identified by name. The information about his suit is extra or nonessential in identifying the person. Therefore, it is set off by commas.

In the following exercises, you will add participial phrases with nonessential information. Therefore, you will set them off with commas. Try this sample exercise.

Sample Exercise

Rewrite the first sentence with the participial phrase from the second sentence inserted right after the noun it modifies. Enclose the participial phrase in commas.

    The lion tamer entered the cage of growling beasts.

    The lion tamer was <u>armed with only a chair and a whip</u>.

The underlined phrase in the second sentence can be used as a participial phrase.

    armed with only a chair and a whip

The participial phrase is inserted into the first sentence right after the noun it modifies (*lion tamer*) and is enclosed in commas.

    The lion tamer, *armed with only a chair and a whip*, entered the cage of growling beasts.

Exercises

In each exercise, rewrite the first sentence with the participial phrase from the second sentence inserted right after the noun it modifies. Enclose the participial phrase in commas.

1. The mountain climbers decided to pitch camp and build a fire.

   The mountain climbers were chilled by strong, cold winds.

2. The Hawks blamed their coach for the loss.

   The Hawks were beaten badly by the Rams.

Sometimes a participial phrase modifying the subject of a sentence can be placed at the beginning of the sentence. Here is an example.

> Walking through the woods, John caught poison ivy.
>
> ↗
>
> comma

Notice that a comma separates a fronted participial phrase from the rest of the sentence. Try this sample exercise.

Sample Exercise

Add the participial phrase from the second sentence to the beginning of the first sentence.

> Kathleen decided to fly to sunny Phoenix for a long weekend.
>
> Kathleen was depressed by the endless rain.

Answer Explanation

Here is the participial phrase from the second sentence.

> *depressed by the endless rain*

This phrase is added with a comma to the beginning of the first sentence.

> *Depressed by the the endless rain*, Kathleen decided to fly to sunny Phoenix for a long weekend.

Exercises

In each exercise add the participial phrase from the second sentence to the beginning of the first sentence. Some of the phrases are past participial phrases and others are present participial phrases. All require commas.

1. Our cat ran and hid under the sofa.

   The cat was frightened by the thunder.

2. Sam accidentally sat on a man's lap.

Sam was trying to find an empty seat in the dark movie theater.

What is wrong with this sentence?

Hanging out to dry in the yard, Paul forgot about the laundry.

The sentence could be interpreted to mean that Paul was hanging out to dry. The problem is that the participial phrase (*hanging out to dry in the yard*) is next to the wrong noun. It should be next to *laundry*.

Paul forgot about the laundry *hanging out to dry in the yard.*

In the incorrect sentence above, the participial phrase is called a "dangling participle." It is "dangling" because it does not seem connected to the noun it is supposed to modify. Avoid dangling participles in your own writing. If you discover a dangling participle when you reread something you have written, correct it. In some cases you can correct a dangling participle by simply moving it. Try this sample exercise.

Sample Exercise

Rewrite this sentence with the participial phrase moved so it does not dangle.

Swinging through the trees, the children enjoyed watching the monkeys.

Answer Explanation

The participial phrase should be moved right after the noun it is meant to modify: *monkeys*.

The children enjoyed watching the monkeys *swinging through the trees.*

Exercises

Rewrite each sentence with the participial phrase moved so it does not dangle.

1. Pacing back and forth in their cages, our children were fascinated by the tigers.

2. Covered with dust, Michelle did not recognize the value of the painting.

Infinitives: The Versatile Verbal

A type of phrase used frequently in English consists of the word *to* and a verb. *To* followed by a verb is called an infinitive. Here are some infinitives.

to eat	to run	to love	to be

Infinitives play various roles in sentences. They can act as subjects and objects in sentences, thus playing the roles of nouns. They can also act as adjectives and adverbs.

Since verbs can have objects and adverbs, the verbs in infinitives can also have objects and adverbs. Here are two examples.

An infinitive along with its adverbs and/or objects is called an infinitive phrase.

Infinitive Phrases
to eat fastidiously
to earn a good living

One use of an infinitive phrase is to express the reason for an action described in a sentence. Here is an example.

Note that a comma is used when this type of infinitive phrase is placed at the beginning of a sentence. Try this sample exercise.

Sample Exercise

Find the infinitive phrase in the second sentence. Then rewrite the first sentence with that infinitive phrase in front.

> Erika stayed home Tuesday evening instead of going out with her friends.

> Erika wanted to finish her term paper.

157

Answer Explanation

Step 1. The infinitive phrase in the second sentence begins with the word *to*. It includes the verb *finish* and the object of the verb (*her term paper*). Here is the infinitive phrase.

to finish her term paper

Step 2. The infinitive phrase is written at the beginning of the first sentence.

comma
↓

To finish her term paper, Erika stayed home Tuesday evening instead of going out with her friends.

Exercise

Find the infinitive phrase in the second sentence. Then rewrite the first sentence with that infinitive phrase in front.

I took a night job as a security guard.

I wanted to earn extra money for a new car.

In the last exercise you added an infinitive phrase expressing a reason to the beginning of a sentence. Such an infinitive phrase often fits well at the end of a sentence also. Here is the answer to the above exercise, followed by another version of the sentence with the infinitive phrase at the end.

To earn extra money for a new car, I took a night job as a security guard.

I took a night job as a security guard *to earn extra money for a new car*.

Note that a comma is not necessary when the infinitive phrase is placed at the end.

Exercise

Find the infinitive phrase in the second sentence. Then rewrite the first sentence with that infinitive phrase at the end.

Myra cuts her hair short every summer.

She wants to feel cooler and more comfortable.

Let us turn now to the use of infinitive phrases for modifying nouns. In the following sentence, the underlined infinitive phrase modifies the noun *person*.

The person *to see about a job* is Marcus Taylor.

The infinitive phrase is said to "modify" the noun *person* because it presents more information about the person. For this reason, it is placed right after the noun *person*.

The above sentence could be constructed by combining the following two sentences.

The person INFINITIVE PHRASE is Marcus Taylor.

He is the person to see about a job.

Here are the steps used in combining the sentences.

Step 1. Find the infinitive phrase in the second sentence.

to see about a job

Step 2. Use this infinitive phrase to replace the words INFINITIVE PHRASE in the first sentence.

The person INFINITIVE PHRASE is Marcus Taylor.
The person *to see about a job* is Marcus Taylor.

Try this sample exercise.

Sample Exercise

Find the infinitive phrase in the second sentence. Then rewrite the first sentence with the words INFINITIVE PHRASE replaced by that infinitive phrase.

In Albuquerque, the place INFINITIVE PHRASE is Fred's Bakery on old Route 66.

It is the place to buy the best bagels.

Answer Explanation

Step 1. Here is the infinitive phrase in the second sentence.

to buy the best bagels

Step 2. This infinitive phrase modifies the noun *place* in the first sentence. It can replace the words INFINITIVE PHRASE.

In Albuquerque, the place *to buy the best bagels* is Fred's Bakery on old Route 66.

159

Exercises

For each exercise, find the infinitive phrase in the second sentence. Then rewrite the first sentence with the words INFINITIVE PHRASE replaced by that infinitive phrase.

1. One of the paintings INFINITIVE PHRASE won first prize at the Newport Art Festival.

    It is the painting to be auctioned this afternoon.

2. Patricia has an opportunity INFINITIVE PHRASE.

    It is an opportunity to obtain a higher paying job.

In the following sentence, the object of the verb is pizza.

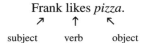

Frank likes *pizza*.

subject　　verb　　object

Note what plays the role of the object in the next sentence.

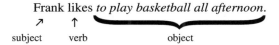

Frank likes *to play basketball all afternoon.*

subject　　verb　　　　　object

In the sentence above, the object is an infinitive phrase (*to play basketball all afternoon*). We could symbolize it like this:

Frank likes INFINITIVE PHRASE.

In the exercises below, you will be presented with two sentences such as these.

Pat decided INFINITIVE PHRASE.

Pat could go bowling tomorrow.

You will create an infinitive phrase from the second sentence. Then you will rewrite the first sentence with the words INFINITIVE PHRASE replaced by the infinitive phrase you created.

To create an infinitive phrase from the second sentence, remember that an infinitive consists of *to* followed by a verb. Therefore, begin by deleting the subject (*Pat*).

~~Pat~~ could go bowling tomorrow.

The word *could* is a modal. An infinitive cannot be formed with a modal:

Wrong: to could

Therefore, the modal *could* should also be deleted.

~~Pat could~~ go bowling tomorrow

An infinitive phrase is created by writing *to* in front of the verb *go*.

to go bowling tomorrow

This infinitive phrase can now replace the words INFINITIVE PHRASE in the first sentence above.

Pat decided INFINITIVE PHRASE.
Pat decided *to go bowling tomorrow.*

Try this sample exercise.

Sample Exercise.

Create an infinitive phrase from the second sentence. Then rewrite the first sentence with the words INFINITIVE PHRASE replaced by the infinitive phrase you created.

Tony hates INFINITIVE PHRASE.
Tony could clean his room.

Answer Explanation

Step 1. First, the subject *Tony* and the modal *could* are deleted from the second sentence.

~~Tony could~~ clean his room

Step 2. *To* is placed in front of the verb *clean* to create an infinitive phrase.

to clean his room

Step 3. This infinitive phrase replaces the words INFINITIVE PHRASE in the first sentence.

Tony hates *to clean his room.*

Exercises

In each exercise, create an infinitive phrase from the second sentence. Then rewrite the first sentence with the words INFINITIVE PHRASE replaced by the infinitive phrase you created.

1. I love INFINITIVE PHRASE.

    I might find my sister's freezer full of ice cream, frozen candy bars, and other treats.

2. My English teacher helped me learn INFINITIVE PHRASE.

    I can write clear, informative sentences.

In the last exercises you used an infinitive phrase as the object of a verb. The object of a verb is usually a noun. Therefore, when an infinitive phrase serves as the object of a verb, it plays the role of a noun.

The subject of a sentence is also usually a noun. But an infinitive phrase may be used as the subject of a sentence when you want to talk about an action. Here is an example.

To stay home and study required will power.

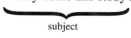

subject

In the following exercises, you will write sentences with infinitives phrases as subjects. Try this sample exercise.

Sample Exercise

Create an infinitive phrase from the second sentence. Then rewrite the first sentence with the words INFINITIVE PHRASE replaced by the infinitive phrase you created.

INFINITIVE PHRASE is Sonja's idea of a great vacation.
Sonja could ski from morning until night for a week.

Answer Explanation

Step 1. First, the subject *Sonja* and the modal *could* are deleted from the second sentence.

~~Sonja could~~ ski from morning until night for a week.

Step 2. *To* is placed in front of the verb *ski* to create an infinitive phrase.

to ski from morning until night for a week

Step 3. This infinitive phrase replaces the words INFINITIVE PHRASE in the first sentence.

To ski from morning until night for a week is Sonja's idea of a great vacation.

Exercises

In each exercise, create an infinitive phrase from the second sentence. Then rewrite the first sentence with the words INFINITIVE PHRASE replaced by the infinitive phrase you created.

1. INFINITIVE PHRASE is unethical.

   Someone could cheat on a test.

2. INFINITIVE PHRASE is to love her.

   You could know my cat.

Placing words between *to* and the verb of an infinitive is called "splitting the infinitive." Here is a sentence with a "split infinitive."

Mr. Wilson decided *to* quickly and secretly *buy* the business.

In this sentence, the phrase *quickly and secretly* splits the infinitive *to buy*. Splitting the infinitive in this way can make a sentence sound awkward. To avoid splitting the infinitive, the phrase *quickly and secretly* could be moved to a different position, such as the end of the sentence.

Mr. Wilson decided to buy the business *quickly and secretly*.

In the following exercises, you will rewrite sentences to eliminate split infinitives. Try this sample exercise.

Sample Exercise

Rewrite this sentence with the word splitting the infinitive moved to the position right after *talk*.

To loudly talk with a friend during a movie is inconsiderate.

Answer Explanation

In this sentence, the infinitive *to talk* is awkwardly split by *loudly*. Therefore, *loudly* should be placed after *talk*.

To talk *loudly* with a friend during a movie is inconsiderate.

Exercises

Rewrite each sentence with the material splitting the infinitive moved to the end.

1. Lou wanted to immediately earn a high salary.

2. The teacher asked Robin to without any further delay turn in his homework assignment.

Many of the above exercises include a grammatical term which students must replace with an actual grammatical structure. For example, students must replace the term GERUND PHRASE in the first of the following sentences with a gerund phrase created from the second sentence.

GERUND PHRASE is an investment in the future of humanity.

subject

People teach children to read.

Such exercises reinforce students' familiarity with grammatical terms, allowing teachers to use the terms when they discuss errors and options in papers that students write.

Furthermore, having students create gerund phrases and embed them in sentences is a more powerful learning experience than merely asking students to underline gerund phrases in sentences, as is done in most traditional grammar texts. If asked only to underline gerund phrases, a student might learn the definition just long enough to do so. In fact, a student could just pick out an *ing* word as the gerund without getting the broader and more meaningful learning that results from transforming a sentence into a gerund phrase by deleting the subject and adding *ing* to the verb.

The teaching of grammar to improve writing skills attains its greatest power when students have an opportunity to practice and master advanced structures such as participles and infinitives. But in traditional grammar, few students get to such advanced structures because they never come to understand the basic concepts. They never practice using gerunds as subjects, participles as modifiers, and infinitives as objects. Instead they just live in confusion about grammar and in fear of grammar tests. It is no wonder that few students develop a fondness and respect for grammar as a valuable friend for helping them express their ideas, attain better grades in various courses, succeed academically, and, in a world where most better-paying jobs now require strong writing skills, prosper professionally.

CHAPTER
19

A PARADIGM SHIFT IN GRAMMAR: THE PROTOTYPE-SPECIFIC MODEL

The term paradigm shift is used by historians of science to refer to the development of a new model for organizing the data in some field of human knowledge. For example, the heliocentric model of the solar system proposed by Copernicus and Galileo was a paradigm shift from the geocentric model of Aristotle and the Scholastics. Aristotle designated the earth to be the center of the universe, with the sun and all the planets revolving around it. But Galileo's telescopic observations convinced him that the situation was quite different. The sun was the stellar hub, and the planets, including the earth, revolved around it. This shift had a profound implication for religion and philosophy: humans could no longer regard themselves as the center of existence but had to accept their position as living on a minor heavenly body that had no particular importance in the greater scheme of the universe.

A paradigm shift has been developing in the field of grammar for some time, and we have extended it in seeking a more accurate theoretical model of English grammar on which to base a more effective pedagogical grammar. For centuries grammar was dominated by a model which maintained that the components of all sentences could be accounted for by eight word classes, called the eight parts of speech: noun, pronoun, adjective, verb, adverb, preposition, conjunction, and interjection. The goal of education in language skills was to teach students how to classify every word of any sentence into these eight categories. Educators believed that in this way students would gain the mastery of English needed to express their ideas in speech and writing.

But two lines of research brought this venerable view into question. Educational researchers found that teaching grammar in this manner— what we have been calling the traditional approach—did not improve students' writing skills. And linguists became increasingly frustrated with trying to fit all the words of sentences into the traditional eight categories. They began to suspect that the age-old model was, like the geocentric theory, not an adequate description of its universe—in this case language. A new model was needed. The new model had to account for what some linguists were calling central and peripheral members of word classes. For example, manner adverbs like *quickly* were regarded as central members of the adverb category. But words referring to time such as *now* and *tomorrow*, which did not describe "how" an action occurred and could not be formed by adding *ly* to an adjective (as *quickly* is formed from *quick*) were peripheral members. In fact, linguists had gone even further in carving up the eight traditional parts of speech. Many felt that articles (*a, an, the*) were too different from typical adjectives to be tossed into the same class. Besides having very different meanings, adjectives and articles behave differently. For example, a pair of adjectives joined by *and* often fits well after the noun they modify:

> The children, hungry *and* sleepy, ate and then went straight to
> bed.   ↖   ↗
>
> adjectives

But articles do not behave in this way. They occur singly and only in front of nouns. Therefore, linguists accorded articles an entirely separate class—a ninth part of speech. Since *a* and *an* are seen as two forms of the same word, with just an inflectional difference to match the sound of the following noun, the ninth word class includes just *a/an* and *the*. This may seem like an unusually small class—having only two specific members. But there are other elements in the language that are also quite specific. An infinitive, for instance, is formed by writing *to* in front of the base form of a verb. But what part of speech is this *to*? Traditional grammarians have called it "the sign of the infinitive," without placing it into any of the traditional eight word classes. In doing this, they have implicitly relegated it to a separate, single-member word class, although they have generally swept this "anomaly" under the rug rather then allowed it into the living area of the other word classes.

The authors noticed that the big word classes, such as verbs, have some members which are exemplary cases, members that might be called "prototypes." Other members of these big classes are nonprototypical in various ways. But there are also small classes with few members, in some cases just one member. These are "specific" elements in the language. In depicting this situation, the authors began referring to the "Prototype-Specific Model' of English when discussing grammar with their colleagues at the TRAC Institute.

The Prototype-Specific Model proved useful in developing a program to teach grammar in a way that provides what DeBeaugrande calls the lower rungs of the ladder, which are needed if typical students are ever to reach a high level of mastery. The model suggested a way of reducing the complexity of grammar in introducing it to students. The model suggested that we begin with prototypes, let students become familiar with the characteristics of prototypes by having them manipulate the prototypes in transforming and constructing sentences, and then move on to nonprototypical cases, more complicated structures, and less general concepts.

For an illustration of how the model was applied in developing the program, consider verbs. The difficulty that traditional grammar has encountered in teaching verbs is described in Chapter 2. To deal with the problem, we first noted that a prototype verb 1. names an action; 2. forms its past tense by adding *d* or *ed* at the end; 3. inflects to agree in number with the subject of a sentence; and 4. occupies the position between the subject and the object of a sentence. The latter two characteristics mean that the only way to illustrate the nature and behavior of a prototype verb fully is to present it in a sentence, an exemplary or "prototype" sentence in which the subject performs an action and the object receives the action:

Prototype Sentence: A car burns fuel.

After students manipulate such sentences to demonstrate inflection for number and tense, they are introduced to nonprototypical verbs. Stative verbs like *own* and *contain* are nonprototypical in not expressing an action. Irregular verbs like *hit* are nonprototypical in a different way. *Hit* does express an action, but it is called irregular because it does not form its past tense in the regular way—by adding *ed*. In fact, *hit* is unusually irregular because its past tense is the same as its present tense:

> Present: Paul and Jack hit home runs regularly.
> Past: Paul and Jack hit home runs yesterday.

Intransitive verbs are nonprototypical in still a third way: they do not pass their action along to an object.

By letting students do exercises in which they inflect these nonprototypical verbs for number and tense in simple sentences, students develop a clear understanding of some primary characteristics of verbs: typical position in a sentence, relationships to other sentence elements, inflection for number and tense, and various meanings besides action.

One verb, however, proved too eccentric to be included in the instructional sequence with the rest of the verbs: the verb *be*. *Be* is the most nonprototypical verb in terms of its form, its meaning, and its behavior (discussed in Chapter 4). Indeed, it is so different from all other verbs that we felt it warranted separate categorization. *Be* forms a distinct class, with itself—in all its glory of numerous forms and uses as a main verb as well as a helping verb in progressive tenses, passive tenses, questions, and negative statements, not to mention its extraordinary impact as part of the infinitive in Shakespeare's immortal "to be or not to be"—being the only member. Therefore, we developed a separate chapter in which students construct sentences with *be* manipulated for changes in tense, number, and person. This is one feature of our P-C workbook that teachers have responded to quite favorably, especially teachers in inner-city schools, where students have trouble with all verbs but especially with *be*.

The Prototype-Specific Model emerged from an ongoing research program attempting to teach grammar more effectively. This goal includes teaching students not just to recognize grammatical structures but also to use them skillfully in constructing sentences. Therefore, the focus of the model is on the components of sentences that students should master for expressing ideas in writing. A case in point is the infinitive. We mentioned earlier that the *to* of the infinitive does not fit into the eight traditional word classes, so traditional grammarians have implicitly categorized it in a separate class called "the sign of the infinitive." But there is an alternative. The verb in an infinitive is not the same type of element as the main verb in a sentence. It never inflects for number or tense. Furthermore, infinitives play totally different roles than main verbs. Therefore, infinitives warrant a separate place in the model. Letting the classes of the Prototype-Specific Model be grammatical structures—components of sentences including words, phrases, and clauses—rather than just words, as in the traditional taxonomy, solves the problem by allowing a class called infinitives to be a part of the model. This is the class of structures that consist of *to* followed by the base form of a verb, along with any objects or modifiers of the verb. In this view, the *to* of the infinitive is not treated as an anomaly that fits nowhere in the eight traditional classes. Nor does it need a separate category. It is part of the major grammatical structure called an infinitive, and it is explicitly mentioned in teaching students about infinitives— their construction, meaning, and placement.

The Prototype-Specific Model recognizes a number of structures that have been studied by linguists but that are not easily handled by the traditional eight parts of speech. An example is an interesting little structure that linguists call a "phrasal verb." The following sentence contains one.

Phil turned on the light.

Traditional grammar would classify *turned* as a verb and *on* as a preposition.

The term *preposition* (*pre*-position) derives its name from the fact that it occurs before (*pre*-) its object. In the above sentence, *on* occurs before its object *light*. The term *preposition* means literally "in the before (*pre*) position."

Generally, a noun phrase like *the light* can be replaced by the pronoun *it*, as in the second sentence below.

The light is too bright.
It is too bright.

But before reading any further, try replacing *the light* with *it* in this sentence.

Phil turned on *the light*.

Is the sentence you constructed idiomatic? Does it sound natural? Is it a correct English sentence? Here is the sentence.

Phil turned on *it*.

This is not an acceptable English sentence—at least not with the meaning of the original sentence. We just don't use sentences of that form. Instead, we place *it* before *on*.

Phil turned *it* on.

But now the preposition *on* follows the object *it*. This unusual position is even clearer when we go back to the original sentence, with the noun *the light*.

Phil turned *the light* on.

When you use the noun phrase *the light*, you can place *on* before or after it. But when you use the preposition *it, on* must come after. Prepositions generally do not act this way. Consider this sentence.

Jim sat on the sofa.

     ↗   ↖

verb   preposition

For this sentence, you cannot move the preposition *on* after its object (*the sofa*).

Wrong: Jim sat the sofa *on*.

Even if you change the noun to a pronoun (*it*), you cannot move the preposition after its objects. Prepositions precede objects.

Wrong: Jim sat it *on*.

Suppose you were trying to explain to a foreign student why *on* can follow *light* but not *sofa*.

Right: Phil turned the light *on*.
Wrong: Jim sat the sofa *on*.

You would have to explain that in the first sentence, *on* is not acting as a normal preposition. And that is exactly what linguists do. In the following sentence, *turned* and *on* are not analyzed as a verb followed by a preposition. Instead, *turned on* is labeled a totally new part of speech: It is a "phrasal verb."

Phil *turned on* the light.

phrasal verb

Furthermore, *turned on* is not a special case. There are many phrasal verbs, another being *put on*.

Ethel *put on* the coat.

Ethel put the coat *on*.

There is another reason for regarding *turn on* in the above sentence as a separate part of speech. Picture Jim as portrayed by this sentence.

Jim sat on the sofa.

On means "above and in physical contact with." Jim is sitting—and he is above and in physical contact with the sofa. But now picture Phil as portrayed in this sentence.

Phil turned on the light.

Is Phil turning—and is he above and in physical contact with the light? Is Phil "on" the light? No. Therefore, in the phrasal verb *turn on*, the word *on* does not have its usual meaning. Having students analyze *turn on* as a verb (*turn*) followed by a preposition (*on*) is misleading with respect to the roles these words play in the sentence. Instead, *turn on* is a separate part of speech, a phrasal verb. In fact, there are additional grammatical reasons for classifying *turn on* and other such combinations as separate parts of speech, but we need not discuss them here. We will simply note that such phrases are allotted their own class in the Prototype-Specific Model. There are, moreover, several other types of phrases that have similar but not identical characteristics to the phrasal verbs we have just examined. Once they have been fully studied, they may be added as subclasses to this category.

Let us examine another interesting phrase, namely, *used to* as illustrated by this sentence.

Claudia *used to* play tennis every morning.

What does *used* mean in the above sentence? Does it have the same meaning as *used* in the next sentence?

Sheila *used* a crowbar to get into the old trunk.

In this sentence, used means "employed" and could be replaced by *employed*.

Sheila *employed* a crowbar to get into the old trunk.

Thus, *used* is a verb and *a crowbar* is its object.

Sheila *used a crowbar* to get into the old trunk.

verb   object

But *employed* cannot replace *used* in the first sentence above.

Wrong: Claudia *employed* to play tennis every morning.

Instead, *used to* is a unit indicating that an activity was engaged in sometime in the past. It means "formerly."

Claudia *formerly played* tennis every morning.

adverb   verb

In the above sentence, *formerly* is an adverb and *played* is the verb. In the next sentence, *play* is the verb. But *used to* is something unique, comparable to the platypus in the animal kingdom, a creature that is somewhat like a mammal and somewhat like a bird or a reptile, but basically unique.

Claudia *used to play* tennis every morning.

platypus   verb

Calling *used to* the platypus of grammatical structures is more than just whimsy. The Prototype-Specific Model of English bears some resemblance to the taxonomy that biologists use for the animal kingdom. For example, zebras and wolves are prototype mammals. Whales and dolphins are also classified as mammals, but they are so nonprototypical that an uninformed observer could be fooled into grouping them with fish. On the other hand, trout and tuna differ even more from prototypical mammals—to such a degree that biologists find it useful to put them into a separate category.

The platypus is classified as a mammal. But it lays eggs, whereas the young of typical mammals are born alive. Furthermore, the term *mammal* is related to *mammary gland*. Mammals produce milk to feed their young. The platypus also produces milk, but while typical mammals have nipples for dispensing the milk, the milk of the platypus just flows out from little holes and gets caught in the fur, from which the young lap it up. There are many other differences. If you have seen a picture of a platypus, you know why it is popularly called the "duckbill" platypus. It has a bill that makes its face look more like that of a duck than that of any typical mammal. Yet, while this little creature does not fit comfortably into any of the major classes of the animal kingdom, its existence has not been ignored nor neglected by biologists. Its characteristics have been fully studied and have provided insights into the developmental relationship between mammals and reptiles.

Similarly, phrasal verbs and *used to* are parts of the language, and a comprehensive model of grammar must give them full recognition. But these structures have found no place among the traditional eight parts of speech. An accurate taxonomy of a real-life domain like living creatures or the grammatical structures of a natural language is likely to be somewhat complicated. The traditional eight parts of speech are an oversimplified representation of English and thus not a very accurate or useful model. As researchers begin to develop a more detailed taxonomy of English, they might find that its form bears some resemblance to that of the animal kingdom, with subclasses accompanied by descriptions of the characteristics that distinguish the members. For example, gerund phrases and noun clauses are used in the noun slots of sentences. Therefore, grammarians might decide to create a new noun category that includes not just single words but also gerund phrases and noun clauses. Single-word common nouns would be the prototypes in this category. Gerund phrases would be one of the nonprototypes, and their distinctive characteristics would be described as fully as those of a subclass in the taxonomy of the animal kingdom.

Special structures like phrasal verbs and *used to* need not be taught in an introductory grammar course. They could be reserved for an advanced course, perhaps an elective course for students who are interested in learning as much about English as possible. This interest might arise from intellectual curiosity. In other cases, it might reflect a desire by future teachers to be fully prepared for teaching English to students coming from homes in which English is not the primary language. Indeed, the need for such teachers is growing, not only because the United States is becoming a multi-cultural nation, but also because English has become the international language of business and scholarship.

But aside from these special structures, there are other, more common grammatical structures that should be taught in every basic two-semester (one academic year) grammar course. Yet these structures have been

173

shortchanged by traditional grammar. Skim through a page from *Newsweek* or *Time* and you will see what a vital role participles, gerunds, and noun clauses play in making sentences interesting—in bringing ideas to life. Then skim through a traditional high school English text and you will see how inadequately these structures are taught. Admittedly gerund phrases and noun clauses are not single words, but they are used in sentence slots often occupied by single words. So, while they do not form word classes, they are parts of speech that form classes of grammatical structures which a pedagogical grammar should fully recognize and teach to students. Consider gerunds. Traditional grammar says they are verb forms used as nouns. But they possess interesting characteristics not shared with nouns. For example, nouns are modified by adjectives. But gerunds can be modified by adjectives or adverbs, as shown in these sentences.

Adjective: *Reckless* skiing is prohibited at this resort.
Adverb: Skiing *recklessly* can cause serious injury and even death.

An adjective placed before a gerund highlights its meaning as a noun, its existence as an "entity." On the other hand, an adverb placed after a gerund helps a reader experience the dynamic (verb) quality of the gerund-its portrayal of action and movement.

In addition, gerunds, unlike nouns, can take objects, allowing a writer to construct sentence subjects of the following type.

gerund phrase

Telling your parents that an "F" on a report card means "fantastic" shows creative imagination, positive thinking, and the mental aberration produced by watching too much TV.

Focusing instruction on the eight parts of speech, and teaching students to classify gerunds as nouns, does not automatically ensure that students learn the different possibilities for modifying gerunds. Similarly, teaching students to classify participles as adjectives may not strengthen a student's facility in using participles to enrich sentences; nor may it help students develop an awareness of the options that a writer has for transforming a dangling participle into a sentence element whose interpretation is unambiguous. We did not present lessons to cultivate such skills and capacities with gerunds and participles in this book because our purpose was simply to show how the P-C Approach introduces advanced structures in a way that helps students understand and use them—a goal not generally achieved by the traditional approach. But experienced teachers can undoubtedly see how they could extend the P-C Approach to teach these useful aspects of gerunds, participles, and other structures. Also, such lessons are included in our advanced workbooks.

By giving full and explicit recognition to structures like gerunds, infinitives, and noun clauses, the Prototype-Specific Model provides the theoretical incentive for teaching students how to construct and utilize them. High school students, many of whom will eventually depend on their writing skills to prosper professionally, can easily learn to handle subordinating conjunctions, relative pronouns, infinitive phrases, and *wh*-word clauses deftly—rather than be intimidated by them. In the words of Chicago teacher Linda Buczyna, students come to view language as a system they can manipulate and master:

> I have been using Whimbey, Linden, and Williams' *Grammar for Improving Writing and Reading Skills* with my 12th-grade students as part of a pilot program with BGF Performance Systems. . . .
>
> I find the program invaluable for meeting objectives in writing, reading, and proofreading. The lessons are well drafted, compact, and to the point. They excel in guiding students to view language as a system they can manipulate and master.

BIBLIOGRAPHY

Baron, Dennis B. *Grammar and Good Taste*. New Haven: Yale University Press, 1982.

Crystal, David. *Cambridge Encyclopedia of Language*. Cambridge and New York City: Cambridge University Press, 1987.

DeBeaugrande, Robert. "Forward to the Basics: Getting Down to Grammar," *College Composition and Communication* 35 (1984): 358-367.

Encyclopedia Americana. 1977.

Gambell, Trevor J. "What High School Teachers Have to Say About Student Writing and Language Across the Curriculum." *English Journal* 73.5 (1984): 23-25.

Greenbaum, Sidney. *College Grammar of English*. White Plains, NY: Longman, 1989.

Greenbaum, Sidney and Randolph Quirk. *Student's Grammar of the English Language*. Harlow, Essex: Longman, 1990.

Hillocks, George, Jr. *Research in Written Composition. Urbana, IL: ERIC Clearinghouse on Reading and Communications Skills/National Conference on Research in English,* 1986.

Lester, Mark. *Grammar in the Classroom*. New York: Macmillan, 1990.

Linden, Myra J., and Arthur Whimbey. *Why Johnny Can't Write*. Mahwah, NJ: Lawrence Erlbaum, 1990. 800-9-books-9

Lochhead, Jack. *Thinkback: User's Guide to Minding the Mind*. Mahway, NJ: Lawrence Erlbaum, 2001.

McCleary, Bill. "Grammar Making a Comeback in Composition Teaching." *Composition Chronicle* 8.6 (1995): 1-4.

McShane, Frank. *Into Eternity: The Life of James Jones: American Writer.* Boston: Houghton Mifflin, 1985.

Merriam Webster's Collegiate Dictionary. 10th ed. 1996.

Morningside Academy. Seattle, WA. <www.morningsideacademy.org>

"Tax Cuts: An Insurance Policy for the Market." *U. S. News & World Report.* March 5, 2001. pp. 58+.

Tchudi, Stephen, and Lee Thomas. "Taking the G-r-r-r Out of Grammar." *English Journal,* 85.7 (1996): 46-58.

Vavra, Ed. "On Not Teaching Grammar." *English Journal,* 85.7 (1996): 32-37.

Vavra, Ed. *Teaching Grammar as a Liberating Art.* <www.pct.edu/courses/evavra>

Whimbey, Arthur. *Mastering Reading through Reasoning.* Raleigh, NC: Innovative Sciences, 1995. 800-243-9169

Whimbey, Arthur and Elizabeth Lynn Jenkins. *Analyze, Organize, Write: A Structured program for Expository Writing.* rev. ed. Mahway, NJ: Lawrence Erlaum, 1987.

Whimbey, Arthur, Myra J. Linden, and Eugene Williams, Sr. *Grammar for Improving Writing & Reading Skills.* Chicago: BGF Performance Systems, 2001. 866-602-1477 <www.bgfperformance.com>

Whimbey, Arthur, Eugene Williams, Sr., and Myra J. Linden. *Keys to Quick Writing Skills: Sentence Combining and Text Reconstruction.* ATP Learning. PO Box 43795, Birmingham, AL 35243.

INDEX

NOTE: The Prototype-Construction Approach to grammar is based on a combination of the authors' research and classroom experiences, not upon the traditional approach of identifying and classifying the eight parts of speech. The format of each chapter presents traditional definitions, examines their drawbacks, and then explains and illustrates the Prototype-Construction definitions of grammatical terms.

Furthermore, the Prototype-Construction Approach works from the simple to the complex in presenting grammatical concepts.

Therefore, P-CA aspects of grammar are not arranged in the same fashion as traditional aspects of grammar. For an outline of the sequence of P-CA aspects of grammar, consult the Table of Contents.

Because of these differences, traditional and prototypical definitions are indicated clearly with the terms "traditional" and P-CA used to distinguish the two.

Starred items *indicate exercises along with explanations of those items.